scribble

COOKIES

And Other
INDEPENDENT CREATIVE
Art Experiences for Children

Written by Mary Ann F. Kohl

Illustrations by Judy McCoy

BRIGHT IDEAS FOR
LEARNING CENTERS

Bright Ring
Publishing

Credits:

Illustrations: Judy McCoy
Cover Design: Scott Montgomery
Typography: Just Your Type

ISBN: 0-935607-10-2

Library of Congress Catalog Card Number: 85-72820

Copyright ©1985 Mary Ann F. Kohl

BRIGHT RING PUBLISHING, P.O. Box 5768, Bellingham, WA 98227

Printed in the United States of America

20 19 18 17 16 15 14

ACKNOWLEDGMENTS

Several excellent teachers have influenced me in my creative teaching: Ellen Fackler gave me enthusiastic support and knowledgeable advice; Chris Johnsen contributed artistic interpretations of favorite projects; and Kris Grinstad demonstrated ideas with fabric.

I thank all the people who have made this book possible: my students of Kindergarten Enrichment and past students of Mountainview School who tried and enjoyed some very unique art experiences; my first principal, Sterling Brand, who encouraged creativity and individuality in all his teachers; and Marlene McCracken who taught me the philosophy that children learn by doing and teachers become successful by guiding children as individuals.

DEDICATION

to my husband, Michael, and
my daughters, Hannah and Megan

Every time we teach a child something,
we keep him from inventing it himself.
On the other hand, that which we allow
him to discover for himself, will
remain with him visible . . . for the rest
of his life.

— Jean Piaget

TABLE OF CONTENTS

FOREWORD

The artistic experiences in this book were developed and compiled for independent expression by children of all ages. Although the experiences in this book are in most cases identical to those used by professional artists, children will explore art and its process, rather than the end product as a goal. Each experience can be set up in an independent art center and enjoyed and explored without adult models to copy. The artist is supplied with materials and technique and left to his own creative expression and exploration. Children will need only to please themselves.

INTRODUCTION

The Independent Art Center

Setting up Your Center "Encourage independence."

Select a corner of the room or a table that will be the center of all your art activities. This will be a "child ready" area with supplies at child level: scissors in a can, pencils, brushes, crayons, glue, tape, stapler, and other commonly used materials. Also keep a supply of paper, newspaper, papertowels, collage items, sewing trims, ink pad, empty cups or dishes, and other items often used on hand. Always keep a "scrap box" clean and filled.

Have a shelf or cupboard nearby at child level. If this is not possible, think in terms of "building" a cubby shelf with shoe boxes, milk cartons, or coffee cans. In all cases, remember that the art center will be dripped and splattered time and time again, so use materials that can be cleaned or materials that can be enjoyed without worry.

Many activities will only need refreshing of materials that are constantly on hand with no adult direction. Other activities will require some time explaining safety and simple techniques. (Under no circumstance should an adult make a model for the child to copy.) Special materials will be set up periodically. Keep the center tidy and clean after each child or group so that other children will come into a center ready for their unique exploration. Of course, children will be responsible for cleaning up after themselves; thus, keep a trash receptical handy, little dust broom and pan, and a tub of soapy water with sponges and hand towels.

Encourage independence! Encourage creativity! ENCOURAGE FUN!

Why A Center? "The art center is a safe place to create."

A center takes the pressure off a child to copy or compete with other children for style, speed, and quantity. A child should be able to work at the art center for as long as he needs, to create as many or as few as he needs, and to create in his own way without a model. The art center is a safe place to create. The art center is also a CREATIVE place to create.

Having an activity ready center benefits the teacher as well as the child. It takes very little preparation to keep a center supplied as compared to setting up a unique project each day. Once a center is established, you need only to set up materials when you wish to add or change an activity. Many new activities can become part of the center's regular supply after the initial introduction for safety or new techniques.

It is also nice to provide a new set of materials and give NO direction but simply watch children create and explore. Children may use these materials as you expect or in entirely new, creative ways. All artistic endeavor has merit. All artists are unique.

Children can move freely from the art center to other centers you might have set up upon completion of the activity. Encourage independence in artistic process, clean-up, and choice of the next activity. Set up independent areas for drying projects, cubbies for work to take home, and a system of choosing activities so that all children have a turn for their choices. A pocket chart for the child's name which he changes as he changes activities works well. If there is room on the chart at a center, then there is room for his name. Centers that are full have no room for names. As an empty space arises, the child may put his name in the space. This encourages independence that is worry free for the teacher and child.

Above all, children succeed because they have worked through the experience and process of art. The end product is not the goal. "Process not Product!"

x

paper

CUT AND PASTE

Arrange an independent center for children to explore. Provide any paper you have on hand and possibly a theme or idea to spark creativity. Many children will wish to create spontaneously. Provide glue in small bottles, paste, glue sticks and tape.

MATERIALS (suggested):

greeting cards	scraps	onion skin paper
wrapping paper shapes	wall paper	tag board
letters	bags	file folders
numerals	newspaper	napkins
magazines	catalogs	construction paper
boxes	art tissue	envelopes
food wrappers	Kleenex	etc.

PRE-CUT PICTURES:

good foods	family	favorites
emotions	colors	pets

THEMES:

emotions	nutrition	family
holidays	alphabet	gifts
children	flowers	a country
litter	counting	love

TORN DESIGN

MATERIALS:
1. scraps of construction paper
2. glue

PROCESS:
1. tear shapes suitable to subject idea
2. arrange on paper
3. glue down

VARIATIONS:
1. designs may bc realistic or random
2. allow children to experiment with tearing before the idea of gluing a finished design is suggested

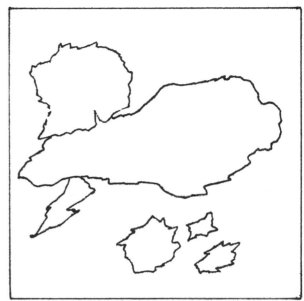
random

realistic

roll

fringe

cut

curl

fold

weave

pleat

3-D EXPERIMENTS

1. scraps of construction paper
2. piece of matt board or sheet of construction paper as a background

PROCESS:
1. encourage children to experiment with paper to make it "stand up" from background
   (possibly look at some of the new paper sculpture books or pop-up books available)
2. children cut, tear, or use scraps as they find them

SUGGESTIONS:
1. colors on a black background are effective
2. some children enjoy building a "bug playground" or "elves' village"
3. provide many shapes and colors

VOCABULARY:

fringe	bend	wad	wrinkle
curl	score	roll	cut
twist	weave	punch	tear
fold	pleat	slit	scrape

The vocabulary could be demonstrated or children may wish to make a demonstration board labeled with each word.

POSITIVE AND NEGATIVE METHOD A

positive

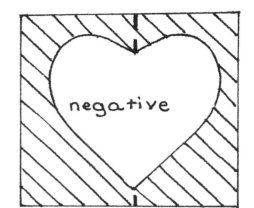

negative

unfold

MATERIALS:
1. scissors
2. construction paper
3. glue

PROCESS:
1. select 2 papers of contrasting colors, one large and the other half that size
2. fold the smaller in half
3. cut a hole or design out of the folded side of the half piece
4. unfold both parts
5. paste both parts on a background paper

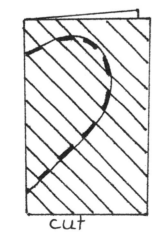

cut

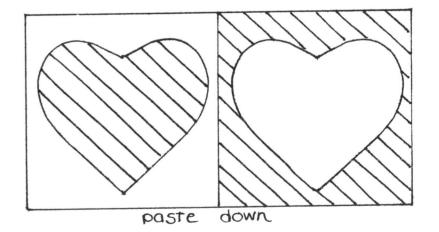

paste down

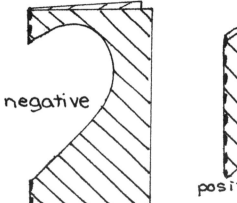
negative

positive

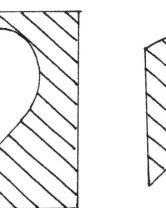
cut apart

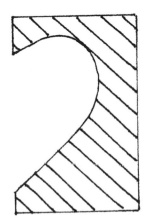
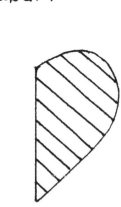

POSITIVE AND NEGATIVE METHOD B

MATERIALS:
same as Method A

PROCESS:
1. cut the positive and negative pieces from Method A in half on the fold
2. paste down these half pieces, alternating the positive and negative

VARIATIONS:
1. cut more than one shape from the folded piece and alternate them on the large paper, keeping them in order
2. try this method with fabric, wall paper, or wrapping paper glued down on cardboard or on a bulletin board

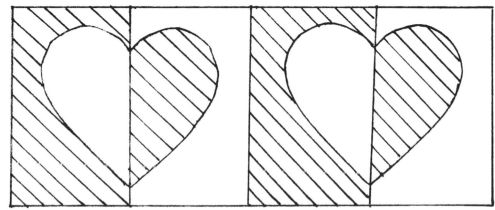
paste down in any interesting design

CONFETTI

MATERIALS:
1. confetti or tiny scraps, and punch-holes saved from paper punch (try the office of a school or a teachers' room)
2. white glue thinned with water
3. brush

PROCESS:
1. brush some thin glue over part of the background paper
2. place or sprinkle confetti on glue area
3. brush with more thin glue
4. proceed until paper is covered in desired fashion

VARIATIONS:
1. identical process can be followed on blocks of wood, glass jars, wax paper, or rocks
2. effective worked over a crayon drawing to resemble snow, magic, outer space

COFFEE FILTER DYEING
dip and dye

MATERIALS:
1. alcohol or water
2. food coloring
3. small bowls
4. coffee filters (look for large, flat filters)

PROCESS:
1. mix in small bowls:
   food coloring with alcohol or water (alcohol dries faster)
2. fold filters in any manner
3. dip into one or more colors and unfold
4. allow to dry

VARIATIONS:
1. try dipping paper towels, napkins, or white wrapping tissue (allow to dry before unfolding)
2. decrease drying time by placing paper in a warm oven or a microwave until dry

SUGGESTIONS:
1. I have found that white wrapping tissue makes a lovely gift when several sheets are folded and wrapped in a box
2. white wrapping tissue, of course, makes good wrapping paper
3. you can buy tiny containers of fabric dye in powder form in most art stores (more brilliant and more variety than food coloring)

TRACING SHAPERS

MATERIALS:
1. tracing paper
2. pencils, crayons, or pens
3. shapes cut from heavier paper

PROCESS:
1. choose any shape
2. lay tracing paper over shape and trace
3. move shape and trace again
4. continue until desired design has been attained
5. design can be further colored or appreciated as is

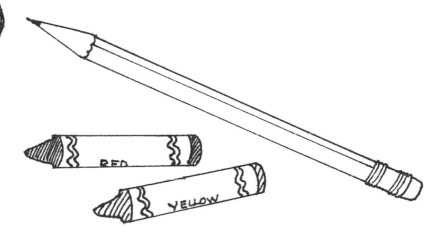

TISSUE BLOSSOMS

MATERIALS:
1. art tissue cut in little squares (about 1")
2. white glue in a dish
3. pencil

PROCESS:
1. push a square of tissue around the end of a pencil
2. holding tissue with fingertips around the pencil, dab tissue into white glue
3. then dab the tissue onto a design or at random on construction paper, tag board, or poster paper
4. for a full solid effect, be sure blossoms touch each other

VARIATIONS:
1. cut large squares of art tissue and wrap around the end of a dowel or block for a large design

SUGGESTIONS:
1. fill in blossoms on a pre-drawn design
2. this project is good for a huge group design with many people contributing blossoms

NEWSPAPER SCULPTURE

MATERIALS:
1. newsprint or newspaper
2. masking tape
3. pencil or ½'' diameter wooden dowel

PROCESS:
To make rolls —
1. lay newsprint on floor
2. beginning at corner, roll paper around pencil by rolling diagonally across paper
3. tape end to form and hold roll
4. shake out pencil
To make sculpture —
1. tape end of roll to table, floor, or poster paper
2. tape another roll to the first roll
3. keep adding rolls

VARIATIONS:
1. try to build a sculpture you can enter
2. try to build a sculpture that moves
3. try to build a sculpture that reaches the ceiling
4. add other materials such as feathers, yarn, rubber bands
5. jump on sculpture upon completion!
6. paint newsprint rolls upon completion
7. use tiny rolls of paper made from 6'' squares of newsprint
8. use very large rolls of paper made from newsprint from the local newspaper company rolled around broomstick
9. excellent group engineering that grows and grows

STRIP ART

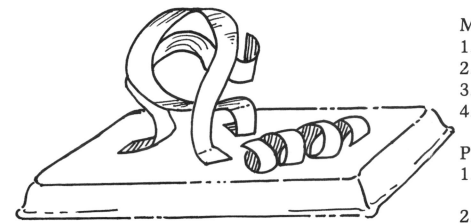

MATERIALS:
1. cut long narrow strips of newspaper
2. glue
3. tempera, brush
4. base (box lid, styrofoam, or wood block)

PROCESS:
1. cut long narrow strips of newspaper and glue 3-4 together
2. let them dry, then paint with tempera or leave plain
3. twist and bend the strips into interlocking shapes
4. glue your sculpture to a base, holding it in place with pins until dry

VARIATIONS:
1. flowers: cut out circles, stack them and attach to florist wire (add leaves, place in vase)
2. thin strips sculpture: twist 3″ paste-coated strips into long ropes, lay on foil, and form and pinch them into shapes like fish, stars, animals (dry, paint, mount on base)

PAPER PLATE COLOR SPIN

MATERIALS:
1. children's record player
2. paper plates with hole in center
3. water based felt pens
4. masking tape

PROCESS:
1. punch hole in center of paper plate with end of scissors or pencil
2. stick a loop of masking tape on back of plate
3. place plate on record player like a record
4. turn on
5. gently touch felt pen to plate as it spins
6. move pen or hold still, experimenting with design
7. turn off record player and remove plate and tape

VARIATIONS:
1. cut other shapes of paper instead of plate
2. experiment with speeds on record player
3. experiment with different types of pens
4. try crayons

COLLAGE

MATERIALS:
1. variety of papers:

wall paper	tissue
colored paper	newspaper
greeting cards	textured paper
wrapping paper	magazine pictures

2. glue or paste
3. scissors
4. background for gluing: cardboard, sheet of paper, old file folder, matt, or box lid

PROCESS:
1. cut and glue in a random or planned approach
2. cover the entire background
3. overlap edges
4. allow collage to dry

VARIATIONS:
1. try for a theme, such as HAPPINESS, CHRISTMAS, NUTRITION, LITTER, PETS, etc., and have all the pictures and paper relate to that theme
2. work as a group and do a huge collage (it's fun to sneak in individual photos of the artists)
3. cover the entire collage with clear contact paper and use for placemats, alphabet search or other games with wash-off felt pen

LETTER COLLÉ

MATERIALS:
1. colored magazine letters, pre-cut
2. scissors
3. paste
4. white or colored paper for background

PROCESS:
1. paste letters on background to create figures, designs, or scenes (combine two or more letters to create these)
2. paste letters in place when satisfied, or create as you paste

DEFINITION:
A collé is a technique in which scraps of paper are pasted to provide decorative and tactile additions.

MAGAZINE COLLÉ

MATERIALS:
1. colored magazine pictures to be used as texture
2. scissors
3. paste
4. sheet of white or colored paper for background

PROCESS:
1. select magazine pictures
2. cut these into shapes which will create a scene or design
3. arrange on background paper
4. paste

SUGGESTION:
Adapt the magazine picture to illustrate a texture, i.e., an illustration of cornflakes could be cut to represent hair, a field, etc.

DEFINITION:
A collé is a technique in which scraps of paper are pasted to provide decorative and tactile additions.

VARIATIONS:
1. paste magazine picture shapes to cover entire background like a collage
2. paste magazine picture shapes without regard to textures but for color or theme, i.e., an entire illustration of flower cutouts pasted to resemble one giant flower, or an illustration of red cutouts to make a Christmas design

PAPER MOSAIC

MATERIALS:
1. scissors
2. colored paper scraps or colored magazine pictures
3. paste or rubber cement
4. hat pin or darning needle
5. pencil
6. background paper or matt

PROCESS:
1. make a light pencil drawing on background paper
2. cut colored paper into small uniform sizes and sort into egg carton by color
3. apply paste to individual pieces and place them on drawing (a hat pin or needle will help in picking up pieces)
4. leave a narrow space of background between the pieces if desired
5. continue pasting

VARIATIONS:
1. try confetti or punched paper for the mosaic pieces
2. try seeds, grain, beans, cereal, popcorn for pieces
3. try a mosaic without a pre-drawn picture for a random or free design

CUT PAPER DESIGN

MATERIALS:
1. thin paper, such as typing paper, and a background paper
2. scissors
3. rubber cement

PROCESS:
1. fold paper into a small square or rectangle
2. cut small shapes and holes out of the paper until there is very little paper remaining
3. carefully unfold
4. cement down on a contrasting background paper

VARIATIONS:
1. try snowflakes
2. try a shape such as a star or heart, flower or apple and then fold and cut
3. try mounting the cutout on a background of wall paper or gift wrap, poster, magazine picture, or original drawing

chalk
and crayon

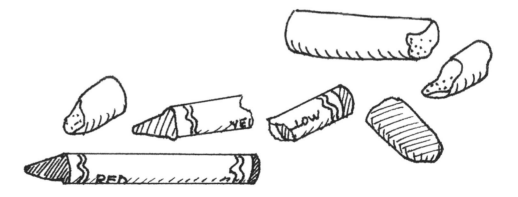

STARCH OR SUGAR CHALK

MATERIALS:
1. colored chalk
2. liquid starch or sugar-water in a cup

PROCESS:
1. dip end of chalk into a cup of liquid starch or sugar-water
2. use like a crayon (very bright—resists smudging)
3. continue dipping and drawing
4. try on a variety of papers and textures

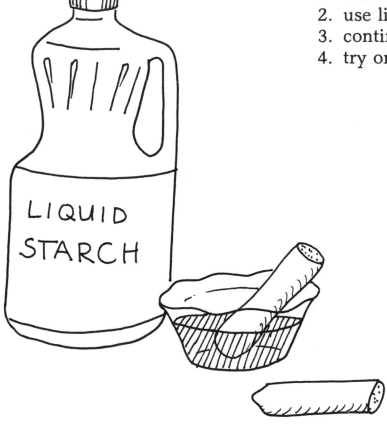

STRING CHALK

MATERIALS:
1. tack or nail
2. wooden board
3. string or yarn
4. colored chalk
5. paper

PROCESS:
1. tie a string to a tack or push pin and push into a wooden board
2. place paper on board
3. tape corners of paper if desired
4. rub string with chalk in a back and forth motion
5. pull the string tight and "snap" against the paper (releases a "poof" of chalk on the paper)
6. continue this process, moving paper about, changing chalk color if desired

VARIATIONS:
1. fill in the areas or shapes created where chalk lines cross over each other
2. use as a background paper for other projects

WET PAPER CHALK

MATERIALS:
1. heavy paper
2. water
3. chalk

PROCESS:
1. dampen heavy paper
2. draw over damp paper with chalk (hint: chalk soaked in sugar-water 10 minutes reduces smearing)
3. allow to dry

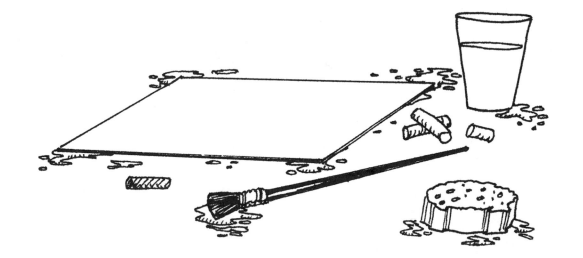

CHALK STENCILS

cut a positive stencil

MATERIALS:
1. squares of tag board or old file folders
2. scissors
3. chalk, paper, facial tissues

PROCESS:
1. cut any shape from a folded square of tag board (you can draw "inside" negative shape or "around" the positive shape)
2. lay stencil (or piece out of the stencil) on a piece of drawing paper and trace around the shape
3. leave stencil in place (hold) and gently brush chalk with tissues
4. remove stencil (effect is soft, muted)
5. repeat as desired

VARIATIONS:
1. try for repetitive pattern
2. try crossing stencils over each other
3. experiment with a variety of colors crossing each other

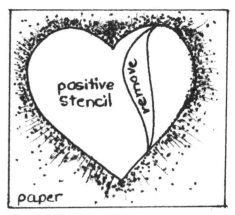

trace outside stencil, brush with tissue, then remove stencil

cut a negative stencil

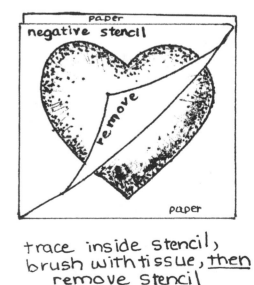

trace inside stencil, brush with tissue, then remove stencil

TRANSFER: CHALK AND CRAYON

MATERIALS:
1. chalk
2. 2 crayons—one white, one any other color
3. paper

PROCESS:
1. apply chalk colors heavily to paper, tapping to remove dust and covering desired area
2. coat these chalk colors with white crayon
3. coat the white with any color crayon
4. turn paper COLORED SIDE DOWN on a piece of smooth paper
5. draw on it with a blunt pencil or a brush handle (press firmly)
6. the chalk and crayon colors will transfer to the smooth paper

WARMING TRAY CRAYON

MATERIALS:
1. warming tray, set on low or med/low
2. foil
3. peeled crayons
4. many types of paper

PROCESS:
1. cover tray with foil
2. a. draw directly on foil and press paper on completed design or b. lay paper on foil and draw on paper, taped at 2 corners
3. crayon melts as it warms while you draw
4. remove paper—hang in window when dry
5. simply wipe off foil with a paper towel for next artist

VARIATIONS:
1. draw on paper plate in an electric fry pan lined with foil
2. try drawing on fabric
3. use little designs glued on folded cards for greeting cards
4. effective for mobiles

SAFETY:
1. one artist at a time
2. hold crayon at end away from heat
3. be sure cord does not stretch across traffic

CRAYON WAX RESIST

MATERIALS:
1. crayon
2. paper
3. paint wash*

PROCESS:
1. draw with crayon on paper using heavy pressure
2. wash over crayon design with a wash of tempera, watercolor, or ink (dark colors such as black, blue, or purple are effective) crayon resists the paint

VARIATIONS:
1. draw with paraffin or a candle
2. scrape through wax or crayon drawing with scissors before putting on the wash for an etched effect

*wash: watered down, thin paint (use a nice soft brush that holds liquid or use a wide brush)

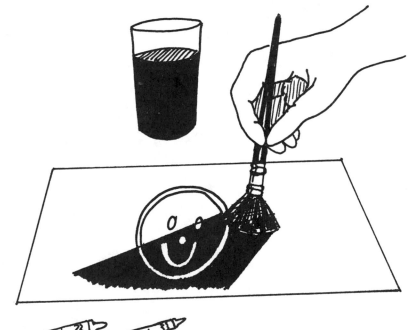

CRAYON RUBBING

MATERIALS:
1. peeled crayons
2. paper
3. objects to use for rubbing (see list of suggestions below)

PROCESS:
1. underlay paper with one or many objects, especially
   flat ones:
   flowers, leaves, other natural objects
   paper shapes
   yarn
   textures, fabrics, cardboard
   coins
   look at surfaces too large to bring to the table:
   walls
   floors
   fence
   grave stone
   manhole cover
   license plate
   bricks
   keyhole
2. lay paper on top of object(s) (hold or tape)
3. rub with long flat side of peeled crayons

WAX
PAPER

WAXTEX

YELLOW

RED

BLUE

LAMINATIONS
melted crayon

MATERIALS:
1. old crayons
2. old cheese grater
3. waxpaper
4. newspaper
5. old iron
6. string, thread, or yarn for hanging

PROCESS:
1. grate crayon onto waxpaper
2. cover with more waxpaper (hint: if you wish to hang completed lamination, now is the time to insert a piece of yarn or thread between waxpapers)
3. cover all of this with newsprint to absorb spills or leaks
4. quickly touch warm iron to the covered waxpaper and shavings (too hot or too much pressure will muddy the design, so start gently)

VARIATIONS:
1. include leaves, yarn, doilies, stickers, cut-outs, etc.
2. lovely mobiles or window decorations
3. mount between paper frames
4. use dry, pressed flowers between the waxpaper with or without the shavings

ENCAUSTIC PAINTING

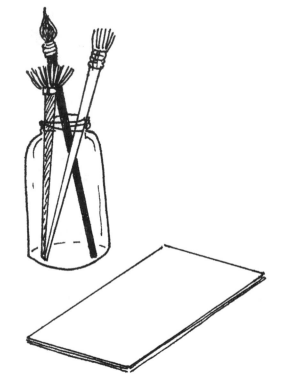

MATERIALS:
1. hot plate or electric frying pan
2. old muffin tin
3. crayon stubs, peeled
4. old paint brushes
5. paper

PROCESS:
1. sort crayon stubs into muffin tin cups
2. melt on hot plate, keeping warm enough to stay liquid (hint: set muffin tin in an electric frying pan lined with foil and set on low)
3. dip brush into color and "paint" (crayon dries thickly as you paint resembling oil painting)
4. mix colors on paper
5. if crayon cools and hardens in tin, re-heat and melt
6. brushes can be cleaned by washing in very hot, soapy water or in dishwasher (these brushes should be forever assigned to wax work)

SAFETY:
1. observe caution around heat and electric cords—one at a time
2. tape down paper for security
3. brace hot areas to prevent tipping or spilling
4. be sure cord is out of traffic and busy elbows

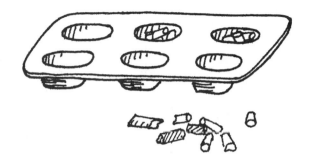

EMBOSSING

MATERIALS:
1. folded newsprint "cushion"
2. paint brush handle
3. paper
4. crayons

PROCESS:
1. place paper on a cushion of folded newsprint
2. "draw" with brush handle deeply into paper, being careful not to tear
3. stroke a light colored crayon back and forth across surface (hint: go gently and leave lines uncolored—if lines are deep enough, the "invisible" design will appear)

VARIATIONS:
1. turn embossed design over, then color, paint, or pen the raised design leaving the rest of the paper untouched
2. place a piece of foil on the newsprint cushion and draw gently with the brush handle—no painting necessary

CRAYON ETCHING

MATERIALS:
1. at least 2 colors of crayon
2. paper
3. cloth or tissue for polishing
4. sharp scissors or plastic knife

PROCESS:
1. cover entire surface of paper with heavy coat of BRIGHT CRAYON(S), avoiding dark colors (free or planned design)
2. crayon over this bright crayon with DARK CRAYON(S) such as black, blue, violet (try to cover ALL the bright crayon)
3. rub surface gently with a cloth or tissue
4. scrape surface through with scissors or knife to the original bright color (experiment with other tools for etching)

ARM DANCING

MATERIALS:
1. large sheet of paper on floor
2. short musical selection
3. crayons

PROCESS:
1. place large piece of paper on floor
2. play a short musical selection of your choice
3. invite child to use a crayon to help do ''arm dancing''
   on paper
4. encourage child to change colors as the music changes
   if he likes

MUSIC: (suggestions)
1. Peer Gynt's HALL OF THE MOUNTAIN KING
2. Tchaikowsky's SUGAR PLUM FAIRY
3. any of John Phillip Sousa's marches

FABRIC CRAYON TRANSFER

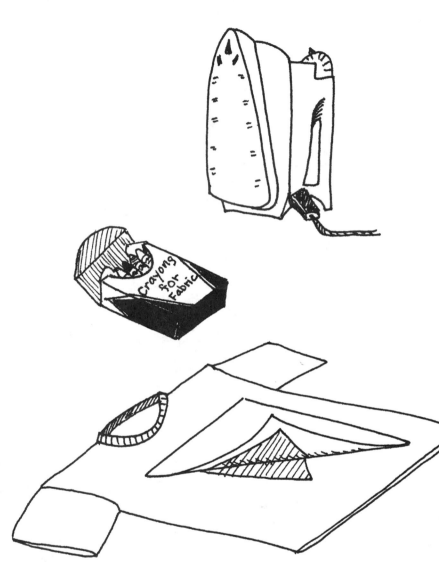

MATERIALS:
1. fabric crayons (available at hobby stores and most variety stores)
2. washed fabric such as 100% cotton
3. plain white paper
4. iron
5. old towel or newsprint to absorb excessive transfer

PROCESS:
1. draw on white paper with fabric crayons (if words or names are used, they MUST be printed in reverse to transfer correctly)
2. lay paper with drawing FACE DOWN on fabric
3. cover with newsprint or old towel
4. press with hot, dry iron (note directions on crayon box)
5. peel away drawing (this transfer can be washed and dried and will retain its bright color)

VARIATIONS:
1. use on pillow cases, T-shirts, quilt squares, puffy picture frames
2. windsox, kites
3. tote bags, back packs, bandanas, belts, head bands

SCRIBBLE COOKIES

MATERIALS:
1. old crayons, peeled (stubs)
2. muffin tin
3. warm oven

PROCESS:
1. save stub ends of old crayons
2. peel and break in pieces
3. sort colors into muffin tin (mixing colors is interesting too)
4. put muffin tin in warm oven turned off
HINT: remove from oven while crayon is squishy but not liquid
5. let melt, then freeze (for easy removal)
6. pop out! (muffin tin washes nicely in very hot, soapy water)

DO NOT EAT!

VARIATIONS:
1. color with scribble cookies as you would any crayon
2. try scribble cookies for—
   encaustic painting, p. 30
   rubbings, p. 27
   embossing, p. 31
   etching, p. 32
   and scribbling!

PROBLEM DRAWINGS

MATERIALS:
Create the following challenges:
hole in paper
any squiggle
any geometric shape glued on paper
any letter
1. the challenge
2. pens, crayons, or paint

PROCESS:
1. let artist incorporate the shape, hole, etc., into a completed work as he draws or paints (some children choose to ignore the challenge or work inside the challenge)
2. use a variety of paper sizes, from very tiny to very large
3. adult CAN take dictations of the artist's story or explanation of his work, but this is certainly in addition to the artistic merit of the experience
4. try this challenge at the paint easel or on the wall

FREE DRAWING

IDEAS: Try these different effects on drawing!
1. provide a variety of PAPERS, SHAPES, COLORS, TEXTURES
2. limit MATERIALS—one crayon and one color paper
     —one paint brush, many paints
     —colored pencils and tiny paper
     —felt pen with opposite color paper (red paper, green pen)
3. try paper in different POSITIONS
     —on the wall
     —at the easel
     —on the table
     —on the floor
     —on a curved surface
     —hanging free in the air from string
     —under a table
     —inside a dark box
4. provide many types of CRAYONS
     —Crayola 64
     —primary
     —jumbo
     —fluorescent
     —peeled
     —scribble cookies
     —flat, shaved
     —stubs, sharpened
     —candles and paraffin

MYSTERY PICTURE

MATERIALS:
1. white crayon or piece of paraffin
2. white paper
3. watercolor paints, brush, water

PROCESS:
1. draw picture with crayon or paraffin on white paper
2. "color in" some areas if desired
3. with watercolor paint (any colors), wash over the paper and watch picture appear like magic

VARIATIONS:
1. draw picture with crayon or paraffin and then trade with a friend for the watercolor step . . . try guessing what the picture is as it appears
2. try using tempera paint
3. try using fingerpaint
4. try dipping entire crayoned picture into a bath of watercolor in a shallow tray
5. try a black crayon on black paper and paint over with white tempera (red on red, white tempera; yellow on yellow, blue tempera; grey on grey, yellow tempera; etc.)

paint

EXPERIPAINT

EXPERIMENT!

TRY—
1. dry paints on wet paper
2. wet paint on wet paper
3. crumpled paper
4. bumpy paper
5. very smooth paper
6. thick and thin paints
7. paint ON: fabric
          wood
          leaves
          rocks
8. paint WITH: large wide brush
          stick
          Q-tip
          cotton ball
          sponge
          feather
          duster
          hands, feet, elbows
          turkey baster
          gadgets, junk
          yarn ball

LET YOUR IMAGINATIONS GO!

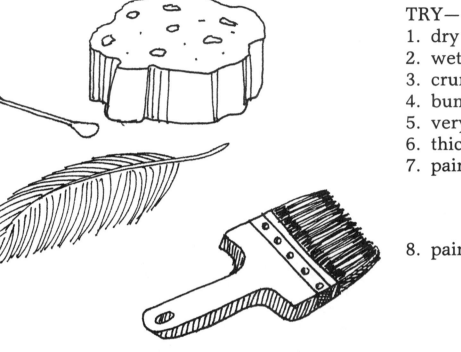

CAR TRACKS

MATERIALS:
1. thick tempera
2. cookie sheet
3. small toy cars
4. paper

PROCESS:
1. pour thick tempera onto a cookie sheet
2. roll small cars through paint
3. drive the cars on a piece of paper, creating designs

VARIATIONS:
1. use dry design play mat for cars
2. drive cars on poster paper on wall
3. experiment with ink pad instead of paint

MARBLE TRACKS

MATERIALS:
1. cake pan or shoe box
2. paper cut to fit pan or box
3. puddle of tempera
4. marble
5. spoon
6. container of water

PROCESS:
1. cut paper to fit pan or box
2. put a puddle of paint on the paper in the pan or box
3. put a marble in the pan or box and roll around by tipping
4. spoon out the marble and plop into a container of water to clean (hint: having lots of marbles available makes this experience run smoothly for larger groups)

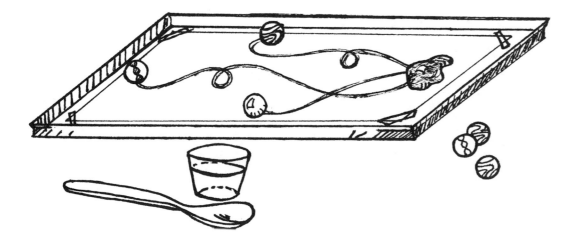

DAMP PAPER
tempera or watercolor

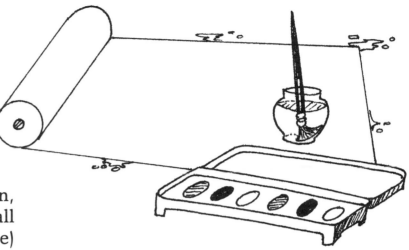

MATERIALS:
1. water
2. any paper (butcher paper is effective)
3. paint, brushes

PROCESS:
1. wet paper entirely under faucet or in large flat pan, with sponge, or with full brush (wrinkle paper in a ball at this time if you wish a batik effect—then unwrinkle)
2. blot off excessive moisture, but paper needs to be shiney wet
3. paint (experiment with dripping, swirling, mixing colors on paper)

VARIATIONS:
1. try shaking dry tempera from a salt shaker onto wet paper
2. use objects other than a paint brush to apply paint (sponge, Q-tip, feather, etc.)

This technique gives a soft, blurry effect.

BLOTTOS

MATERIALS:
1. fairly thick tempera paint
2. spoon or brush
3. pre-folded paper

PROCESS:
1. drop or brush thick blobs of tempera paint on the fold or one side of the paper
2. fold over and press gently
3. unfold (note symmetry)

VARIATIONS:
1. cut out when dry and use for flowers, butterflies, bugs, monsters, or lovely designs
2. glue on a pipecleaner and put in a vase
3. use as a mural of creatures or a garden
4. try for heart shapes, people, butterflies, frogs, or other symmetrical designs

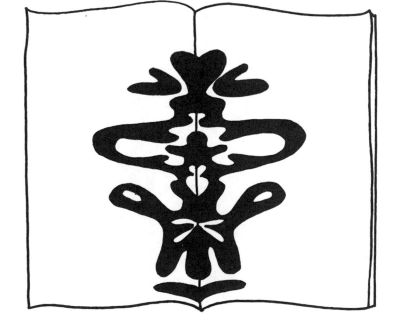

WATERCOLOR SALT

MATERIALS:
1. white glue in bottle
2. watercolor paint box with brush
3. jar of water
4. any paper — white is effective
5. salt in spout container
6. empty cup

PROCESS:
1. "draw" with white glue from bottle
2. pour salt on glue drawing
3. pour extra salt from drawing into a cup to be used for other drawings with glue
4. paint salt and glue with watercolor paint, using a minimum of water
5. rinse brush between colors if you wish
6. allow to dry

VARIATIONS:
1. brush glue onto paper from a dish for a variety of line widths and thicknesses
2. very effective for rainbows and sunsets
3. experiment with watercolor salt on other surfaces such as wood, styrofoam, and cardboard

RUNNING COLOR

MATERIALS:
1. thin tempera
2. brush or spoon
3. paper

PROCESS:
1. using a very thin tempera, apply in spots or drops to paper
2. turn paper this way and that, letting paint run in different directions
3. let colors cross each other and make new shades

VARIATIONS:
1. apply to paper by dipping a straw in paint and holding dry end with a finger to hold paint in straw
2. change colors often to experiment with the mixing of colors as they cross over each other
3. use a turkey baster on a large sheet of paper, tipping table or board to run the colors

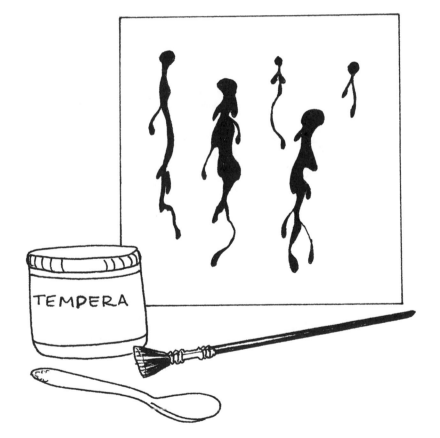

SQUEEZING COLOR

MATERIALS:
1. empty containers from ketchup, mustard, liquid hand soap, shampoo, or dish detergent
2. tempera paint of medium consistency
3. paper

PROCESS:
1. fill empty containers with paint
2. squeeze paint on to paper

VARIATIONS:
1. this activity is effective on a very large surface or on a vertical surface (wall)
2. try a turkey baster on a large surface

BLOWING COLOR

MATERIALS:
1. thin tempera paint
2. spoon, brush, or straw

PROCESS:
1. drop a puddle of paint on paper using a spoon, brush, or straw
2. using a straw, blow on the puddle forcing the paint in any direction or creating a sprayed effect
3. colors may be mixed or simply use one color

VARIATIONS:
1. try this on paper hung on a wall
2. use a turkey baster instead of a straw on a large paper
3. try other liquids such as—
   ink
   food coloring
   water on dry tempera paint sprinkled on paper
   experiment with other ideas and materials

PUFFY PAINT

MATERIALS:
1. equal parts of flour, salt, and water
2. bowl, spoon
3. liquid tempera paint to desired color
4. cardboard squares or heavy paper
5. plastic squeeze bottles such as mustard or ketchup containers

PROCESS:
1. mix equal parts of flour, salt, and water in a bowl
2. add liquid tempera paint for color in desired amount
3. pour into plastic squeeze bottles
4. squeeze mixture onto cardboard or heavy paper
5. mixture will harden in a puffy shape
6. colors will pool together without mixing
7. allow experimentation in design and pattern

SPLATTER

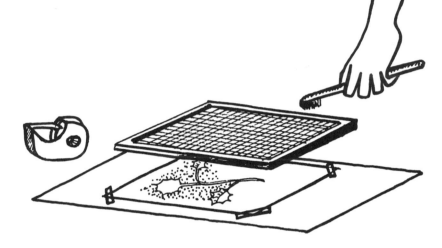

MATERIALS:
1. tempera paint
2. paper
3. small piece of window screen
4. toothbrush
5. tape
6. newsprint
7. objects of nature or cut-out shapes

PROCESS:
1. tape paper in center of newsprint
2. arrange leaves or cut-outs on paper
3. pick up small amount of paint on the toothbrush
4. hold screen above paper and rub toothbrush back and forth across the screen to make splatters
5. remove shapes or leaves and dry

VARIATIONS:
1. experiment on scrap paper or newspaper to get the idea
2. try other objects such as scissors, a fork, a bracklet, kitchen utensils, tools, or anything washable that will leave a nice, stenciled outline
3. splatters make nice greeting cards or wrapping paper
4. try an entire mural or picture using cut-outs that make a scene, tell a story, or create a unique design or pattern
5. create a fairy tale in splatters or a favorite book

WATERCOLOR STAINED GLASS

MATERIALS:
1. box of watercolor paints with brush
2. jar of water
3. paper
4. permanent black felt pen

PROCESS:
1. paint with watercolors on paper
2. covering entire paper can be effective
3. allow to dry
4. when dry, choose parts of painting to trace or outline with black felt pen

VARIATIONS:
1. draw with pen first, then watercolor paint the design or picture
2. experiment with other felt pen colors
3. try using water based felt pens on the wet painting

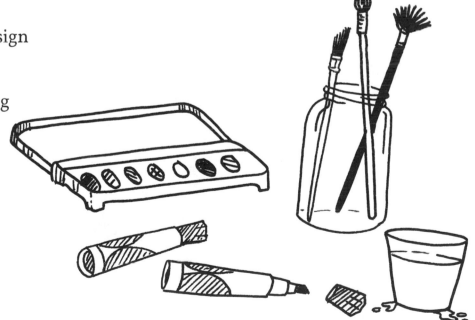

PULLED STRING

MATERIALS:
1. yarn or string
2. dish of tempera
3. construction paper or drawing paper
4. rag or sponge, damp

PROCESS:
1. dip string or yarn into dish of tempera paint
2. do not squeeze paint out of string
3. lay string on a sheet of paper in any design, leaving the tail end of string off the edge of the paper
4. place another piece of paper over this
5. lay hand gently over paper and string
6. pull string from paper, keeping hand pressing gently
7. remove top paper and observe designs

VARIATIONS:
1. try a folded sheet of paper and place string inside
2. try several colors, one at a time, adding each color after the first is done
3. try a rope dipped in paint and place between very large sheets of paper (many hands can help)

SHINY PAINT

MATERIALS:
1. tempera paint, liquid or powdered
2. white glue
3. cups, brushes

PROCESS:
1. pour white glue into cups
2. mix your choices of tempera paint colors into each cup, stirring with a brush
   HINT: if you use powdered paint, you may have to thin mixture with a little water to paint easily
3. paint on wood, paper, cardboard as you would with any paint
4. paint will dry shiny as if glazed

VARIATIONS:
1. when dry, glaze entire painting with white glue thinned with water for an extra layer of clear glaze
2. paint pine cones, rocks, driftwood, glass
3. try painting with sponge brushes from hardware store for a very smooth finish
4. to help paint adhere to shiny, smooth surfaces, add a few drops of dish detergent to paint/glue mixture

WET FELT PENS

MATERIALS:
1. water base felt pens
2. heavy drawing paper, fingerpaint paper, or tag board (smooth papers work nicely)
3. water, jar
4. soft brush

PROCESS:
1. draw with felt pen
2. using a wet brush, "paint" over felt pen lines (performs much like "paint with water" books or water colors)

HINT:
1. fresh felt pen lines paint better than very dry ones
2. use wet brush frequently instead of waiting until the end of the drawing

RUBBER CEMENT RESIST

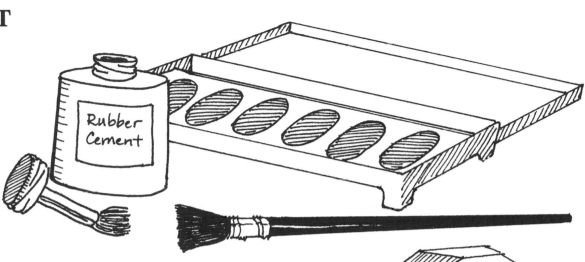

MATERIALS:
1. watercolor paints with brush
2. paper
3. rubber cement with brush
4. eraser

PROCESS:
1. paint a picture with rubber cement using the brush attached to the jar or with a finger
2. rubber cement must dry
3. paint over the rubber cement with watercolor paint (rubber cement will resist the paint)
4. allow the paint to dry
5. rub away the rubber cement with the eraser and the original paper or drawing will be exposed

VARIATIONS:
1. do this over areas previously painted and repeat as often as you desire (be sure each layer is dry before applying the next)
2. try this on commercial wrapping paper or a poster but use tempera paint

FINGERPAINTING OVER CRAYON

MATERIALS:
1. drawing paper
2. liquid starch
3. tempera powder
4. crayons

PROCESS:
1. cover the paper with bright crayon
2. spread liquid starch over crayon
3. sprinkle powdered tempera over starch (contrast the paint with the crayon)
4. move hands over paint and starch and mix
5. fingerpaint
6. dry

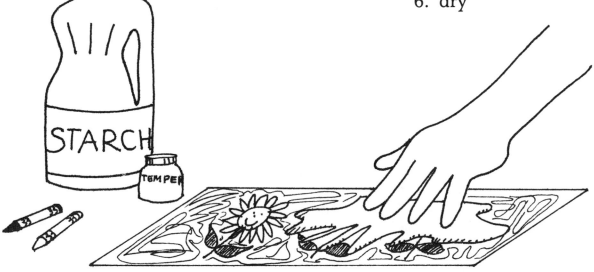

SILHOUETTE PAINTING

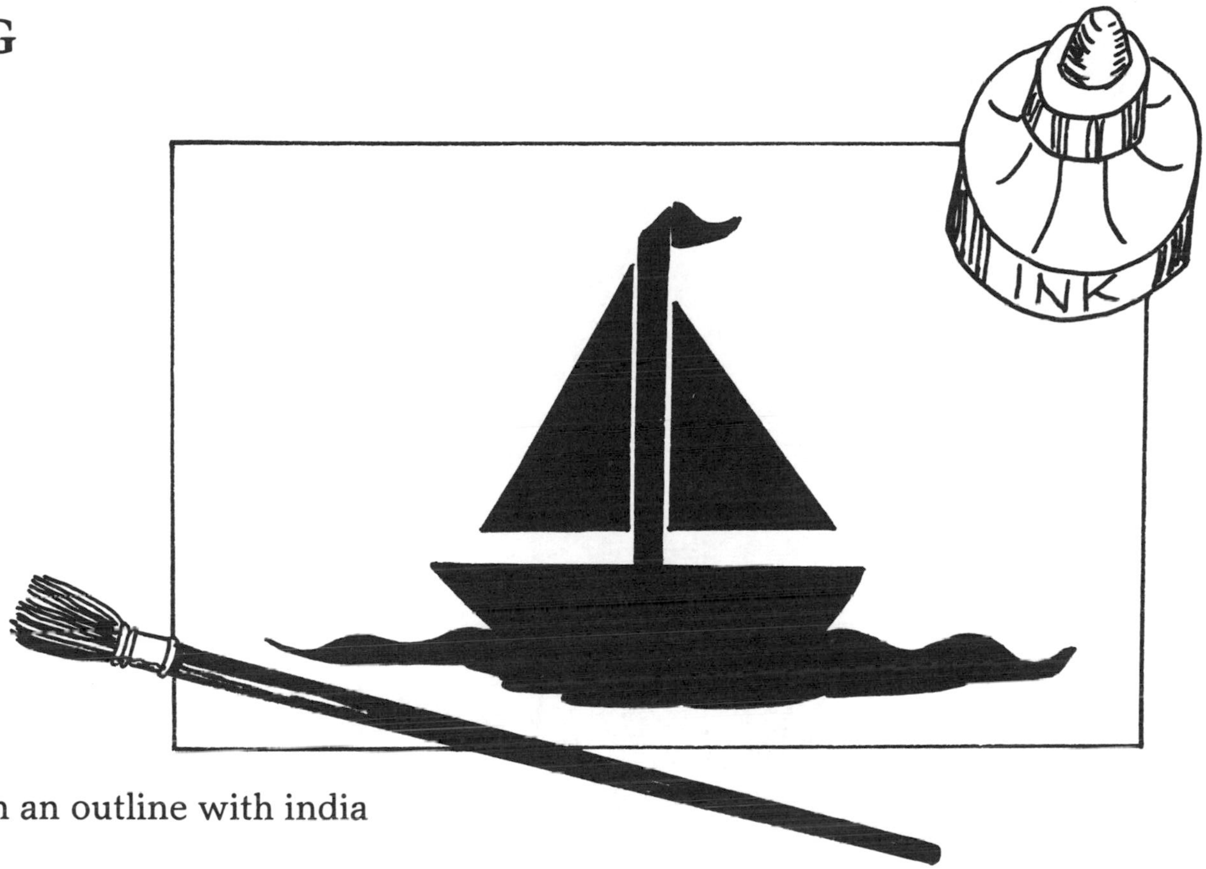

MATERIALS:
1. black ink or paint
2. brush
3. paper
4. scissors

PROCESS:
1. paint an entire shape rather than an outline with india ink or black paint
2. keep bold and simple
3. sketch a drawing first if desired
4. fill in entire shape

VARIATIONS:
1. paint a sunset with tempera or watercolor and when dry, add a silhouette of trees, mountains, desert, or any figures or scenery desired
2. cut out silhouettes and paste on a background paper, drawing, or painting

SALT PAINTING

MATERIALS:
1. liquid starch
2. paper plate, matt board, or cardboard
3. water
4. tempera or food coloring
5. brushes
6. salt

PROCESS:
1. mix:
   1/8 C. liquid starch, 1/8 C. water, and 1 T. tempera or 2 squirts food coloring, plus 1/2 C. table salt
2. apply mixture to background with a brush
3. keep stirring mixture
4. painting will crystalize as it dries

TISSUE FINGERPAINTING

MATERIALS:
1. liquid starch
2. powdered tempera
3. shiney paper
4. torn or cut-out tissue paper shapes
5. glue thinned with water, brush

PROCESS:
1. drop a puddle of starch on shiney paper
2. sprinkle with powdered tempera
3. draw hand through paint and mix on paper
4. fingerpaint
5. while still wet, press down torn or cut-out art tissue
   paper shapes in any design (if you overlap shapes, add
   a little more fingerpaint between them)
6. brush over design with thinned white glue

VARIATIONS:
1. try sprinkling glitter into glue
2. try pressing doilies or facial tissue into paint

printing

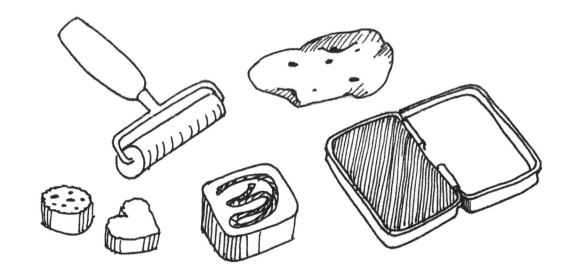

BUBBLE PRINT

MATERIALS:
1. solution of equal parts water and dish detergent
2. small container (baby food jar)
3. food color or tempera
4. pan
5. straws
6. different kinds and shapes of paper

PROCESS:
1. prepare a solution of equal parts water and dish detergent
2. fill small container
3. add food coloring or tempera for desired color
4. set jar in a pan
5. blow with a straw into jar until bubbles mound over the sides (hint: if you cut a little hole in the straw it will prevent "drinking" the solution but will not disturb the blowing)
6. take a print by lightly touching paper to bubbles (as bubbles pop! an imprint is left)

VARIATIONS:
1. try large container of mixture and larger tube for straw

SPONGE PRINTING

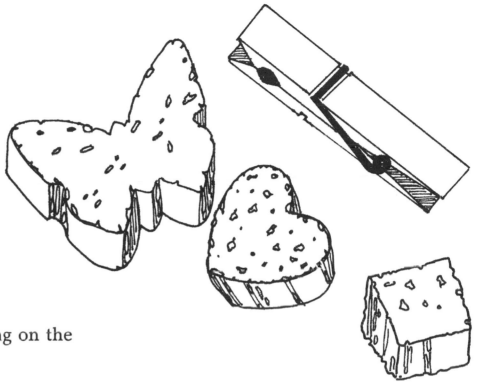

MATERIALS:
1. sponge shapes or squares
2. clothespins
3. paint on a pad or papertowels in a plate
4. newspaper

PROCESS:
1. cut designs in sponges or use squares
2. pinch sponge with clothespin for handle
3. dip in paint, or paints
4. dab on paper for a sponge print

VARIATIONS:
1. try sketching a pencil line design and printing on the design
2. make wrapping paper
3. try blossoms or leaves
4. use for texture on a large mural (grass, fields, sky, etc.)

STRING BLOCK PRINTING

MATERIALS:
1. heavy string
2. white glue
3. block of wood
4. tempera paint on a sponge or ink pad
5. paper

PROCESS:
1. dip heavy string in glue and arrange on a block of wood and dry (string may be arranged in designs, shapes, letters, etc.)
2. press dried block on a sponge with tempera paint for a stamp pad or dip in a plate of paint (ink stamp pads also work)
3. press on paper

VARIATIONS:
1. brush paint onto the block with a brush
2. use for wrapping paper
3. use for a border for a bulletin board

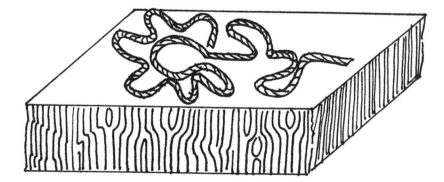

STRING ROLLER OR WOOD PRINT

MATERIALS:
1. white glue
2. yarn or heavy string
3. cardboard tube (heavy) or block of wood
4. paper
5. cushion of newspaper
6. paint, brush

PROCESS:
1. trail glue around a heavy cardboard tube or block
2. push string into the trail
3. dry completely
4. brush paint on the string
5. roll tube on paper or press block on paper
6. experiment with colors
7. experiment with continuous design with the tube

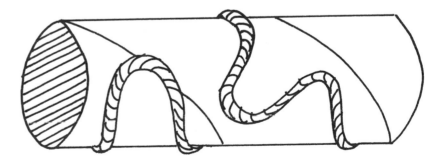

WOOD BLOCK PRINT

MATERIALS:
1. block of wood with raised grain
2. ink pad or tempera paint, brush
3. paper

PROCESS:
1. brush thin paint onto a rough side of a block of wood
2. press the block onto a piece of paper (try twisting or sliding the wood)

VARIATIONS:
1. use blocks of different shapes
2. glue cardboard shapes into block first and dry, then print
3. glue yarn or string onto the block first and dry, then print

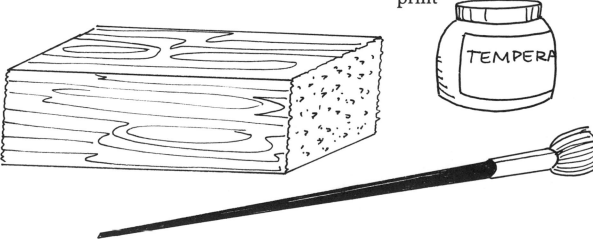

TURPENTINES

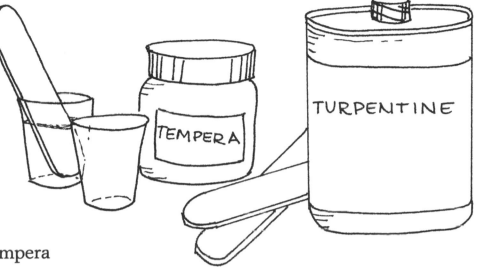

MATERIALS:
1. shallow tray
2. turpentine
3. tempera powder
4. water
5. glass cups
6. paper
7. non-plastic stirring stick or spoon

PROCESS:
1. pour water into a shallow tray
2. in separate cup, mix turpentine with powdered tempera
3. dribble paint mixture onto surface of the water
4. watch patterns—stir to add swirls
5. gently lay a piece of paper over a pattern and lift off (resembles oil in puddles on the street)
6. dry
7. repeat with additional colors and turpentine
8. spray with fixatif if desired

VARIATIONS:
1. try spraying or dribbling oil base enamel paint into a bucket of water and follow the same print process

JUNK PAINTING

MATERIALS:
1. junk:

penny	plastic cup	cookie cutter
spool	domino	checker
nuts, bolts	bottle cap	baby bath toy letters
sponge	seashells	wooden ABC blocks
plastic toy	kitchen items	jar lid

2. paint
3. brush
4. paper
5. newspaper

PROCESS:
1. press any junk or interesting items into paint, or brush the junk with paint (try using an ink stamp pad . . . they come in a variety of colors, even rainbow)
2. print on paper
3. experiment with designs, patterns, or scenes

BRAYER, GLASS PAINTING

MATERIALS:
1. brayer (or a rolling pin)
2. paint with a few drops of liquid detergent added
3. glass (cover edges with duct tape for safety)
4. paper

PROCESS:
1. lay string or any flat objects on table
2. cover with paper, tape 2 corners if desired
3. roll brayer over puddle of paint on glass (or cookie sheet or any smooth surface)
4. roll paint covered brayer across paper
5. change paint color and objects under paper as desired

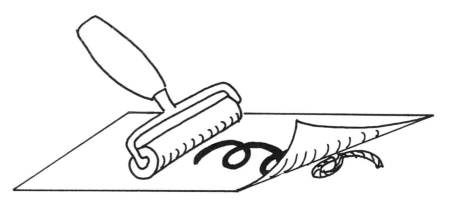

CLAY PRINT

MATERIALS:
1. ball of plasticine clay
2. stick, pencil, plastic knife, nail, or other tools
3. paint brush
4. paint
5. paper

PROCESS:
1. gently push ball of clay against flat surface or table
2. decorate the flattened side with grooves, holes, designs
3. brush on thin paint to designed clay surface (or press clay onto a pad of paint or ink stamp pad)
4. print

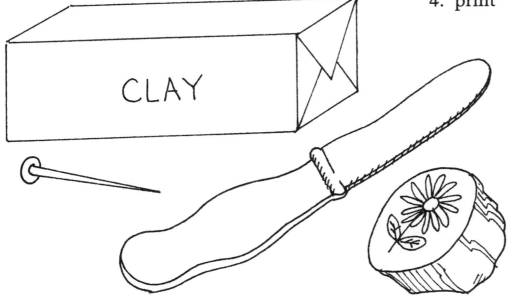

STYROFOAM PRINTS

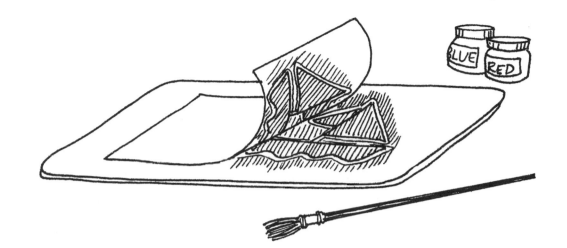

MATERIALS:
1. styrofoam grocery trays
2. pencil or ballpoint pen
3. tempera paint
4. paper
5. paint brush or roller
6. scissors
7. glue

PROCESS:
1. cut off the edges of a styrofoam tray
2. draw a design or picture on the SMOOTH side of the tray, pressing hard with a pencil or ballpoint pen
3. cover picture with paint
4. carefully lay a piece of paper over the painted surface
5. smooth over it several times with your hand
6. pull off the paper (remember that children *will discover* letters and words must be written in reverse)

VARIATIONS:
1. experiment by using several colors at one time
2. try making holiday cards or thank you cards
3. make a set of cards for a gift
4. nice for programs or posters

MONOGRAPH

MATERIALS:
1. smooth surface (table, glass, cookie sheet)
2. paint
3. paper
4. pencil or paint brush

PROCESS:
1. cover a surface with paint
2. lay a paper over this, very gently
3. now with heavy pressure, draw on this paper with a sharpened pencil or the end of a paint brush
4. peel off

EFFECT:
This is similar to fingerpainting on the table and then pressing a paper over the fingerpainting and peeling off.

RELIEF PRINTS

MATERIALS:
1. glue
2. cardboard or block of wood
3. cardboard, scissors
4. paint pad (paint on sponge or pad of paper towels in dish)
5. paint brush

PROCESS:
1. cut a cardboard shape and glue on a piece of cardboard or block of wood
2. allow to dry completely
3. brush paint on the shape or press into paint pad
4. press painted shape down on a piece of paper (or roll over cardboard with a rolling pin)

INK PAD PRINT

MATERIALS:
1. paper
2. ink pad (in any color)
3. newspapers
4. junk and gadgets small enough to fit ink pad

PROCESS:
1. place a pad of newspaper under the paper to be printed
2. press junk, gadgets, fingers, coins, etc., onto the pad
3. press the inked object onto the printing paper (one inking should provide more than one print)

SUGGESTED ITEMS FOR PRINTING:

paper clip	jar lids	kitchen utensils
coin	plastic bag ties	rubber stamps
nail	sticks	domino
old jewelry	wire whip	corks
leaves	fork	checker
pencil erasers	nuts and bolts	any flat items

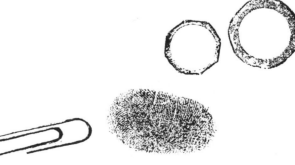

POTATO OR VEGETABLE PRINT

MATERIALS:
1. potato
2. cutting tool (pencil, scissors, nail)
3. knife
4. paper (construction, drawing, tissue, newsprint, brown wrap)
5. paint brush, paint (any kind)
6. water, jar, newsprint
7. tray for mixing
8. rag for clean-up

PROCESS:
1. cut potato in half
2. scratch, cut, or dig design into potato
3. cover the design with paint with a brush or dip into a styrofoam tray filled with paint
4. press potato onto paper which is on a cushion of news-print
5. continue printing (try printing on a scrap of paper to get the idea)
6. different colors may be used, mixing on the potato

VARIATIONS:
1. carrots, turnips, rutabagas, and parsnips may be cut like potatoes and used for printing
2. lovely prints can be made from halved artichokes, cabbage, celery heart, corn on the cob, celery sticks, citrus, etc.
3. use this experience for wrapping paper, cards, decorations, place cards, bulletin board cover paper or borders

MONO-PRINT FROM FINGERPAINTING

MATERIALS:
1. tempera paint
2. liquid starch
3. smooth flat surface (table top, glass, cookie sheet)
4. paper
5. newspaper

PROCESS:
1. fingerpaint directly on the flat surface mixing a little liquid starch and some tempera paint
2. lay a piece of paper on the wet fingerpainting and rub gently with hand until the painting is transferred
3. lift and allow to dry on newspaper
4. when the print has dried, place it face down and iron

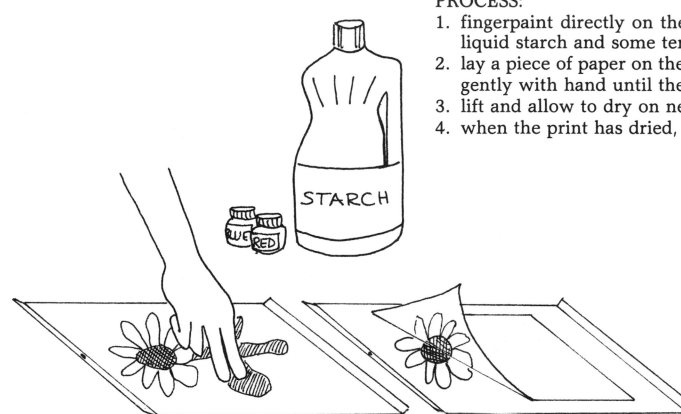

LEAF PRINT

MATERIALS:
1. carbon paper
2. newsprint
3. paper
4. newspaper
5. electric iron
6. green leaves

PROCESS:
1. place a sheet of carbon paper over a leaf, carbon side down
2. press the iron on the carbon paper until the leaf is covered with carbon (certain leaves will need more than one pressing)
3. place leaf on a piece of paper with carbon side down and press until transferred

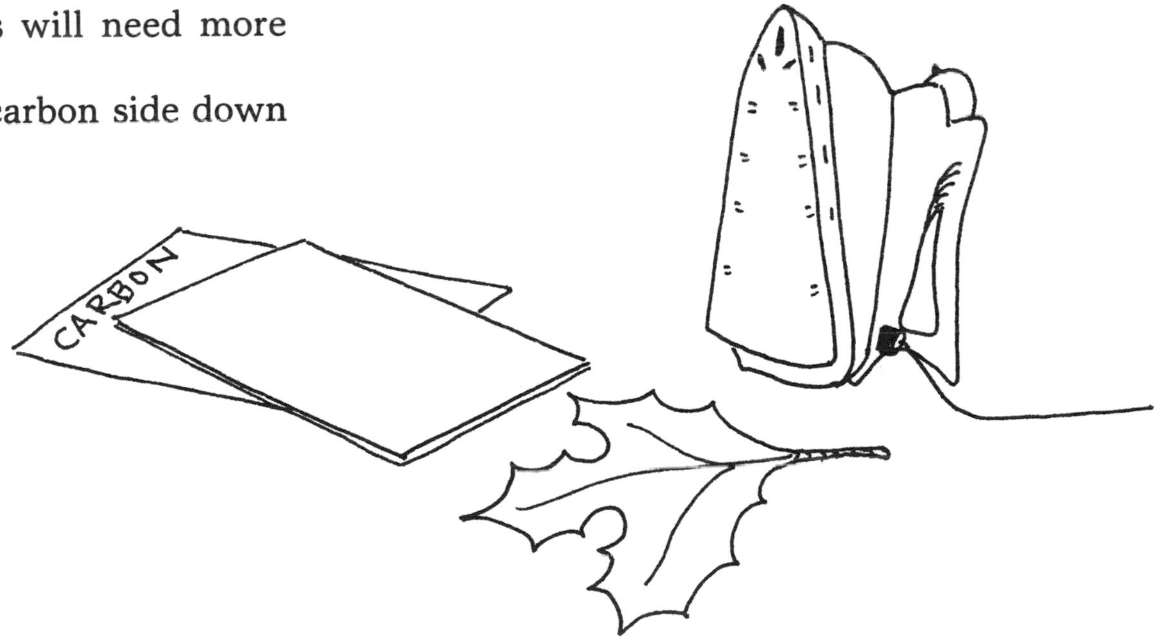

CUT STYROFOAM PRINT

MATERIALS:
1. white styrofoam grocery tray
2. scissors
3. dowel, yogurt "push-up" stick, or block of wood
4. glue
5. paper, ink pad

PROCESS:
1. cut styrofoam grocery tray into shapes, designs, or patterns
2. glue piece onto the end of a dowel, yogurt push-up stick, or small block of wood for easier handling
3. allow to dry at least overnight
4. press styrofoam into ink pad (or into tempera paint on a pad of paper towels in a dish)
5. print on paper

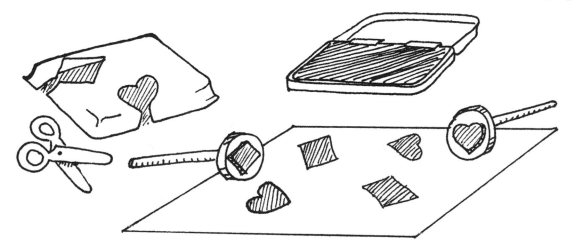

FINGERPRINTS

MATERIALS:
1. fingertips
2. ink stamp pad or paint or felt pens
3. paper

PROCESS:
1. press fingertip onto a stamp pad
2. press inked fingertip onto a piece of paper
3. make designs, patterns, shapes, etc.
4. decorate with felt pen for details if desired

VARIATIONS:
1. use a felt pen to color fingertip and then press onto paper
2. it's fun to use felt pen and decorate the prints to look like flowers, bugs, characters, pets, creatures, etc.
3. nice border for a greeting card

GLUE PRINTING

MATERIALS:
1. white glue
2. heavy cardboard
3. thick tempera paint
4. spoon
5. paper

PROCESS:
1. use bottle of white glue to make a design on heavy cardboard
2. allow to dry (at least overnight)
3. spread with thick tempera paint
4. place paper over the design
5. rub with a spoon to make the print

sculpture
and ceramics

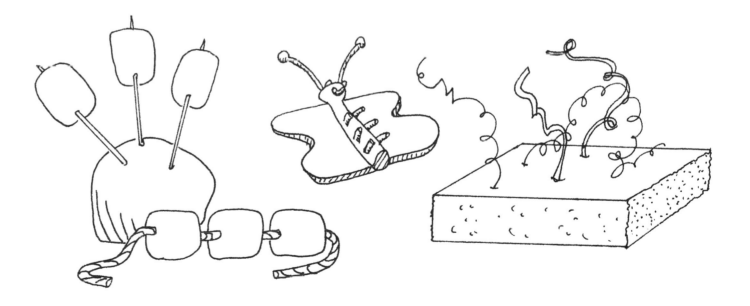

SALT AND FLOUR BEADS

MATERIALS:
1. 1 C. each salt, flour
2. 1 T. alum
3. water to consistency of dough
4. dry tempera or food coloring
5. toothpicks

PROCESS:
1. mix salt, flour, and alum to consistency of putty with water
2. tempera or food coloring may be added for color
3. pinch off and shape into a bead
4. punch hole for stringing with toothpick
5. leave on toothpick sticking in a ball of dough until dry
6. shellac beads if desired
7. string beads on elastic cord, thread, or string

VARIATIONS:
1. instead of beads, try making other things from this dough
2. try coloring with felt pens or watercolor paints when dry

SAWDUST MODELING

MATERIALS:
1. sawdust
2. wheat paste
3. water
4. bowls, spoons
5. measuring cups

PROCESS:
1. mix 4 cups sawdust plus 1 cup wheat paste plus 2½ cups water (add color if you choose)
2. mix and play, explore
3. mixture will harden and dry
4. paint when dry if desired
5. spray with clear enamel if shine is desired

CORNSTARCH DOUGH

MIXTURE:
1 C. salt   ½ C. boiling water
1 C. cornstarch   optional tempera or food coloring

MATERIALS:
1. salt, cornstarch, boiling water, coloring
2. bowls
3. pan, stove
4. spoons, measuring spoons
5. cups
6. optional paints and brushes

PROCESS:
1. mix the salt, cornstarch and water in pan
2. heat over low, stirring until mixture is too stiff to stir
3. when cool, knead until smooth
4. if coloring was not added, dough will be white (paint dough when dry)

GOOP

MATERIALS:
1. ½ C. cornstarch
2. ¼ C. water
3. color (food coloring or tempera)
4. trays, bowls, spoons

PROCESS:
1. mix cornstarch and water and color (you can make a whole water-table full keeping the ratio of cornstarch to water 2:1)
2. pour onto trays or into a tub
3. observe and explore
4. no finished product—just exploration
5. keep reusing mixture (can be stored in a tight container)

VARIATIONS:
1. add more cornstarch and explore
2. add more water and explore
3. try other colorings such as kool-aid or jell-o

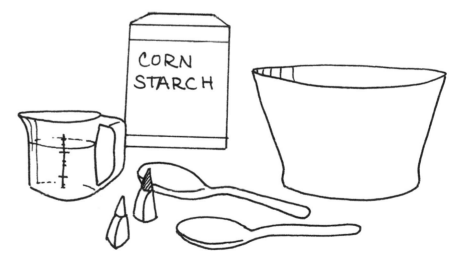

FLOUR AND WATER DOUGH

MATERIALS:
1. 1 Cup flour
2. ½ Cup water
3. food coloring or tempera
4. spoons, cups, bowls

PROCESS:
1. mix flour, water, coloring or tempera
2. stir
3. play, explore, mold, pound, etc.
4. mix more as necessary

DO NOT MAKE MODELS FOR CHILDREN TO COPY,
UNLESS YOU ARE COPYING THEIRS!!

PLAY CLAY

MATERIALS:
1. clay, plasticine modeling
2. tools
3. table

PROCESS:
1. set out piles of clay on table
2. explore with hands (PLEASE do not make models for children to copy)
3. next time add tools to the exploration
4. try pounding, smashing, coiling, rolling, squeezing, pinching, etc.
5. store clay in plastic bags or container with snap-on lid

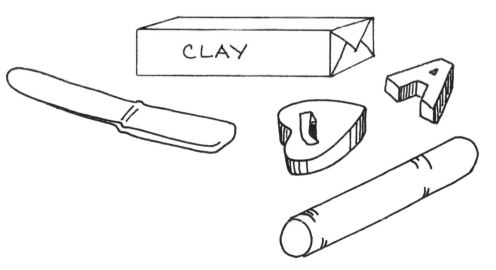

SODA AND CORNSTARCH DOUGH

MATERIALS:
1. cornstarch
2. baking soda
3. water
4. pan, spoon, stove
5. rolling pin
6. food coloring or tempera

PROCESS:
1. combine: 1 Cup cornstarch
            2 Cups baking soda
            1¼ Cups water
2. cook medium, stirring constantly
3. knead when doughlike
4. food coloring or tempera may be worked in when it has cooled some
5. roll out or cut in shapes or model
6. let dry 24-48 hours until hard
7. paint with tempera or watercolors
8. may be shellaced or brushed with clear nail polish
9. mount pins, clips, hangers with white glue
10. keep dough covered when not in use

PLAY DOUGH
(my favorite)

MATERIALS:
Mix and cook on LOW until ball forms, then knead:

1 Cup flour	1 T. cream of tartar
1 Cup water	food coloring, tempera powder,
1 Cup salt	jello or kool-aid

PROCESS:
1. simply give child utensils and a comfortable place to work
2. store dough in snap-on plastic container or coffee can

SUGGESTIONS:

magnetic letters	garlic press
cookie cutters	Tupperware shape ball
knife	screws, nuts, bolts
rolling pin	fork
dowel for rolling pin	VARIETY of utensils

VARIATIONS:
your imagination is the limit

NO ART PROGRAM IS COMPLETE WITHOUT THE
INFORMALITY OF PLAY DOUGH

CLAY RELIEF

MATERIALS:
1. modeling clay, plasticine
2. small tools
3. background: matt board, table, paper, cookie sheet, etc.

PROCESS:
1. make a clay picture, thinking of clay as a three-dimensional paint or drawing
2. stick pieces of clay on a background (no glue because clay sticks to itself)
3. try some texture by stamping clay with small tools
4. leave some areas plain for contrast

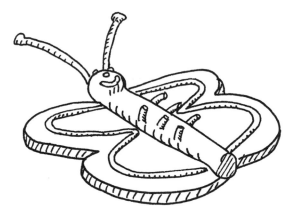

STRAW AND TOOTHPICK CONSTRUCTIONS

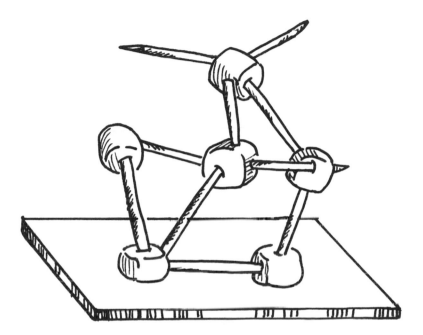

MATERIALS:
1. toothpicks or straws
2. construction paper
3. tissue paper or cellophane, optional
4. tempera paints
5. glue
6. dried peas (soaked overnight), dough, corks, bits of styrofoam, marshmallows, or gum drops
7. scissors
8. crayons

PROCESS:
1. join the straws or toothpicks together with bits of soaked peas, dough, corks, styrofoam, marshmallows, gum drops, etc.
2. a box lid or styrofoam tray could serve as a base, or construction paper

VARIATIONS:
1. glue toothpicks together to make sculptures, dry, paint
2. cut out art tissue in a shape and outline the shape with glued on toothpicks; hang or tape in a window (cellophane is very bright and sturdy in this experience)

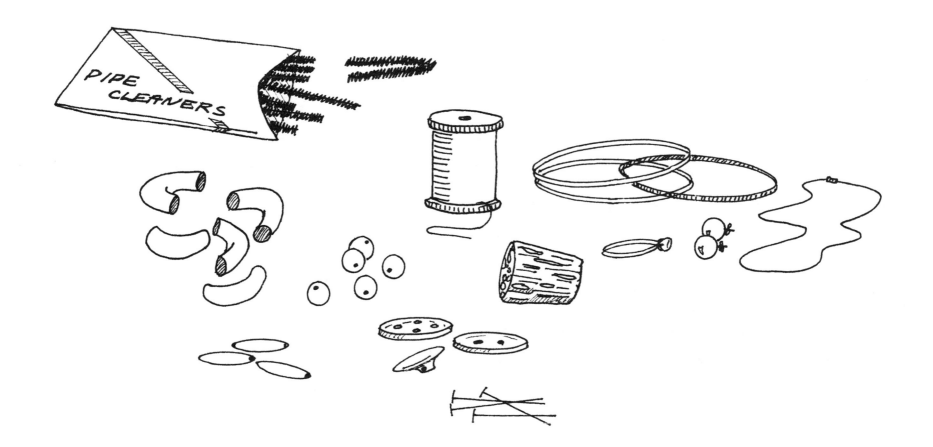

PIPE CLEANERS

STYROFOAM SCULPTURE

MATERIALS:
1. block of styrofoam, such as stereos are packed in
2. variety of items to stick into styrofoam

pipe cleaners	jewelry	skewers	yarn
wire	chains	corks	macaroni
dowels	beads	straws	flowers
thread	feathers	nails	craft sticks
broom straws	toothpicks	screws	

PROCESS:
1. stick any items into a block of styrofoam
2. one large block can be done as a group sculpture

VARIATIONS:
1. weave fabric strips, ribbons, fibers into the sculpture
2. put together and take apart many times

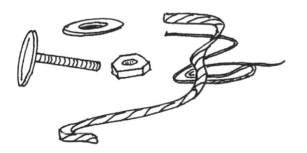

BOX SCULPTURE

MATERIALS:
1. assortment of cardboard, wooden, or metal containers

   oatmeal   liquor case   pizza
   jewelry   coffee cans   Chinese food
   hoisery   milk cartons   shoe
2. white glue
3. tape, stapler
4. paint if desired

PROCESS:
1. collect an assortment of boxes or containers
2. glue, tape, and staple boxes together letting the sculpture take shape as you go
3. paint if desired

VARIATIONS:
1. a group can do a sculpture together
2. try totem poles
   hats
   animals
   instruments
3. try a sculpture with just little containers
4. try a sculpture that touches the ceiling

WOOD SCRAP SCULPTURE

MATERIALS:
1. assortment of wood scraps
   construction pieces
   framing scraps
   shop class scraps
2. white glue
3. paint or crayons if you choose

PROCESS:
1. begin with a base piece and glue each new piece on as you go
2. when satisfied with sculpture, pieces may be painted or colored

VARIATIONS:
1. build the entire sculpture and then go back and glue
2. try letting a group build a "city"
3. individuals make one sculpture on a heavy matt, which can then be assembled as one large display sculpture made up of many single sculptures

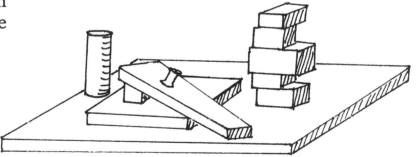

NATURAL OBJECT SCULPTURE

MATERIALS:
1. objects of natural materials (see list)
2. glue
3. paint
4. colored paper
5. spray fixitif

LIST:

seeds	feathers	nuts	dry flowers
twigs	stones	dry grass	shells
pinecones	seed pods	dry weeds	beach glass

PROCESS:
1. collect natural materials
2. arrange to create a small sculpture
3. glue
4. paint or colored paper can be added
5. spray to preserve finish

VARIATIONS:
1. glue shells and glass to a flat rock for a beach theme
2. use a styrofoam tray for a gluing surface
3. cover a matt with burlap or felt and glue materials to fabric
4. glue materials to a block of wood or driftwood piece

WIRE SCULPTURE

MATERIALS:
1. any wire with flexibility
   heavy stove pipe, copper, aluminum, bailing wire, insulated telephone wires in colors
2. scissors or wire cutter
3. styrofoam block

PROCESS:
1. bend and twist wire to desired shapes (experiment with coiling around cylinders, cubes, triangles)
2. stick one end of the wire into a chunk of styrofoam such as stereos are packed in (feed the wire deep into the styrofoam to hold well)
3. for a firm hold, push wire all the way through styrofoam and knot on back side

VARIATIONS:
1. attach wire to nails or screws that have been hammered or screwed into a block of wood
2. check with the telephone company for a large scrap of cable which when opened reveals a rainbow of wires
3. add junk, gadgets, or any collage type items to the wire (buttons, feathers, nuts, beads, hair rollers, keys, spools)

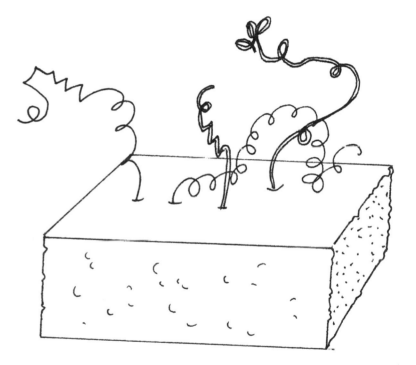

FOIL SCULPTURE

MATERIALS:
1. aluminum foil
2. tape or pins

PROCESS:
1. crumple heavy aluminum foil into any forms or shapes
2. join multiple forms with tape or pins (try to make one sculpture out of one large piece instead of joining several small pieces)

VARIATIONS:
1. add paper sculpture into the crumpling of foil
2. join many forms into one large display

crafts

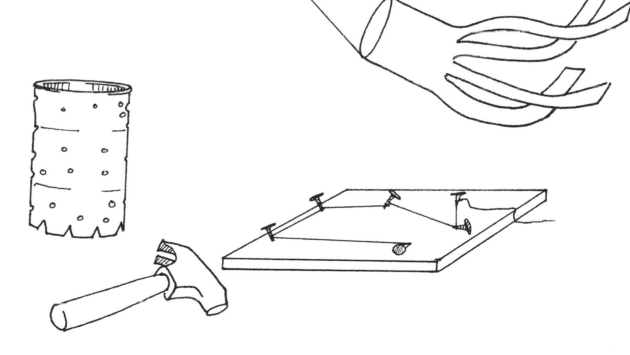

PROJECTOR SLIDES

MATERIALS:
1. slide glass 3¼'' x 4'' (2 pieces for each slide)
2. india ink, watercolor, or transparent ink
3. pen or brush
4. paper
5. paste or rubber cement
6. scraps of cloth or colored cellophane paper
7. paper, tape
8. scissors, knife, or single-edged razor blade
9. pieces of cardboard

PROCESS:
1. make a drawing on a piece of paper the size of the slide glass (include lettering if you wish)
2. place slide glass over the drawing
3. trace outline of drawing with ink using pen or brush
4. add color by painting on the glass with watercolors or ink (hint: very intense colors are achieved when colored cellophane is glued on the slide glass) (textures are achieved by pasting thin pieces of sheer fabric in desired areas)
5. place second slide glass over the finished work and tape the edges to bind
6. show on a 3¼'' x 4'' slide projector or an overhead projector

SUGGESTIONS:
1. this is a challenging project, so allow artists to explore and experiment
2. try this technique on plastic mylar squares to show on an overhead projector experimenting with transparent tissue, fabrics, cellophane, watercolor felt pens

DESIGN BOARD

MATERIALS:
1. square of plywood (8x8 is a nice size)
2. nails with heads, hammer
3. rubber bands, yarn, thread, string, sewing trims
4. other items such as feathers, buttons, stickers, etc.

PROCESS:
1. hammer nails into plywood square in any design (be careful nails do not go all the way through)
2. weave, tie, and connect the nails with colored threads, yarn, fabrics, rubber bands, etc.
3. add any little pretties for design

VARIATIONS:
1. board can be covered first with fabric, painted, or covered with wallpaper
2. add a flip-top from an aluminum beverage can by nailing it on the back and hang design board as a picture or wall sculpture
3. use a variety of wood shapes and sizes
4. glue tiny chunks of framing scraps on the board with other materials above

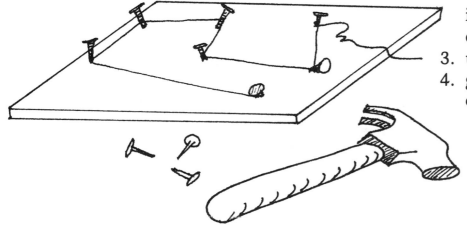

WINDSOX OR STREAMERS

MATERIALS:
1. bright, lightweight cloth
2. needle, thread
3. embroidery hoop or flexible twig

PROCESS:
1. sew a fabric rectangle in a tube shape (fabric should be large enough to reach around the hoop or twig)
2. sew the tube to an embroidery hoop or flexible twig tied in a circle (these can be tied ahead of time and in a box)
3. tear from the bottom up as far as you like, leaving some area near the top intact
4. attach string to hoop if you wish to hang in the wind

VARIATIONS:
1. tiny windsox can be made on keychain rings, but must be snipped with scissors instead of torn
2. decorate fabric with fabric crayons
3. draw on fabric with permanent felt pens

BLEACH OUT

MATERIALS:
1. 1 Cup bleach mixed with 1 quart water
2. denim scraps
3. eye droppers

PROCESS:
1. mix bleach and water in a steady bowl, or pour into individual containers
2. drop from eye dropper onto denim
3. create designs and patterns

VARIATIONS:
1. try a "reverse tie dye" approach by tying denim with string or rubber bands, twisting, and dipping in bleach mixture
2. make a large group banner, flag, or cover a bulletin board
3. make head bands
4. work on old jeans that can be worn for fun

STENCILING ON FABRIC

MATERIALS:
1. clear contact paper
2. scissors
3. fabric, such as unbleached muslin, old sheets
4. fabric paints or fabric chalk

PROCESS:
1. cut out shapes from contact paper
2. peel protective backing
3. stick on fabric, pressing edges down
4. using fabric paints, paint fabric
5. follow paint instructions to set color

VARIATIONS:
1. try for negative stencils by painting inside the stencil
2. try for positive stencils by painting around the stencil
3. try this technique by cutting paper shapes and rubber cementing them to paper, paint or color, then remove shapes
4. try spatter painting the fabric paint with a toothbrush rubbed across a piece of window screen using the contact paper stencils

negative (inside)   positive (outside)

INSTANT BATIK

MATERIALS:
1. unbleached muslin or old sheets
2. pencil, old paint brushes
3. newsprint
4. melted crayon mixed with paraffin
5. old muffin tin
6. warming tray or electric frying pan

PROCESS:
1. draw any pattern or design on fabric with pencil (design should totally fill the space)
2. place fabric on several layers of newsprint
3. melt peeled crayons and paraffin in muffin tin in electric frying pan on LOW or on a warming tray
4. USE CAUTION WITH MELTED CRAYON AND ELECTRIC CORDS
5. paint the melted crayon mixture onto the fabric until it saturates the fabric (if the wax doesn't soak through, paint on the opposite side of the fabric too)

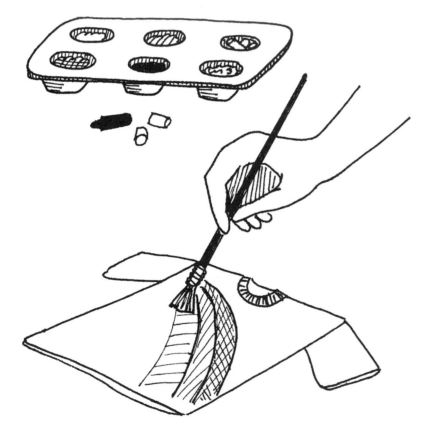

HINT:
the brightest colors seem to give the best results as they
tend to lighten after dyeing and removing wax
6. when dry, remove any wax

SAFE HEATING DEVICE:
A. 1. separate crayons into muffin tin cups by color,
      removing paper
   2. place muffin tin over a cake pan partially filled with
      water and heated over a hot-plate
   USE SUPERVISION AT ALL TIMES
B. 1. find a 2 gallon rectangular can from a service station
   2. cut a hole, large enough to hold the muffin tin
   3. punch a hole about one-quarter of an inch in diam-
      eter through the cap or end of the can
   4. insert an electric cord through the hole and attach
      a socket and 100-150 watt light bulb to one end,
      and an electric plug to the other
   5. heat from the light bulb is enough to melt crayon
      and keep liquid as it is being used

GOD'S EYE

MATERIALS:
1. 2 sticks of equal length
2. yarn
3. scissors

PROCESS:
1. cross two sticks
2. begin wrapping yarn at center of cross
3. as you wrap say: "around and under, around and under"
4. continue in same direction
5. change colors at any time, tying one color to the next
6. tie at the end and tuck in
7. hang

VARIATIONS:
1. add tassles to ends of sticks
2. use tongue depressors and glue at the cross
3. try very large sticks or dowels, secured at the cross and use fibers, rope, heavy yarn for the wrapping (you can also tuck in feathers, sew on beads, and a wide variety of imaginative alternatives)

LANTERNS

MATERIALS:
1. water, a freezer
2. coffee cans, or other cans from soup, fruit, vegetables
3. nails, hammers

PROCESS:
1. fill the can to be used with water and freeze overnight
2. while frozen, hammer a nail around the can making holes (the ice makes this very safe and easy)
3. make several holes in the side around the bottom rim to draw air
4. drain, dry
5. can can be painted or colored with permanent felt pens
6. add a candle and light

VARIATIONS:
1. nail the candle to the bottom of the lantern for security
2. holes can be punched in the side from the top rim and wires attached for hanging
3. themes of design can be hammered for holiday or party lanterns
4. names are fun to hammer

PIÑATAS

MATERIALS:
1. balloon
2. newspaper 1'' wide
3. liquid starch
4. art tissue or crepe paper in sheets

PROCESS:
1. blow up balloon (or a punch ball for a large pinata)
2. tear strips of newspaper approximately 1'' wide
3. dip strips in liquid starch, pulling the strips through your fingers to remove any excess starch
4. cover balloon completely with paper strips, trying to have just one layer of paper over balloon
5. dry
6. to decorate: cut approximately 4'' wide strips of colored tissue paper
7. fold the strips crosswise several times, and then lengthwise once
8. cut this strip so that you have a ''frill''
9. then unfold the strip and glue strips around the balloon starting at the bottom
10. cut open the finished, dry piñata to fill and tie
11. does anyone want to break this open?

WEAVING WITH PAPER

MATERIALS:
1. construction paper
2. scissors
3. paper cutter for adult
4. tape or stapler

PROCESS:
1. fold paper as shown
2. make cuts, straight or wiggly, from the fold (stop at least an inch or more from the edge)
3. unfold paper
4. cut strips of construction paper ahead of time on paper cutter, any width
5. weave strips of paper through cuts (remember children as beginners will use a random weaving style before they discover "weaving")
6. push strips together tightly if desired
7. glue end, staple or tape

VARIATIONS:
1. try this on a paper plate
2. try for a definite pattern (ex. over one, under two, over one, under two)
3. use contrasting colors or papers other than construction paper
4. laminate and use for placemats (or cover with clear contact paper)

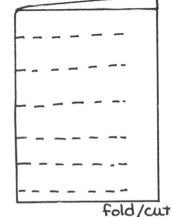
fold/cut

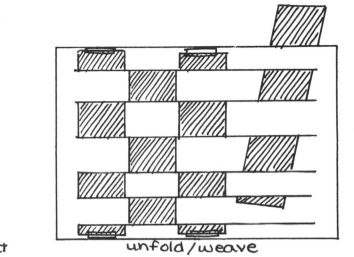
unfold/weave

wiggly cut

paper plate

COLLAGE

MATERIALS:
1. styrofoam tray, paper, fabric, or cardboard
2. glue
3. anything from the list of collage items

PROCESS:
1. glue items onto chosen surface, filling gaps and spaces
2. dry

VARIATIONS:
1. use a "theme" for the collage such as: shapes, seasons, emotions, plants, colors, fun, nutrition
2. try for a group collage with everyone participating on a very large surface

COLLAGE IDEAS:
(see list)

Materials for Collage and Construction

Listed below are some suggestions to help you make a collection of materials to use for collage and construction and for other art projects. From this list you may want to select items to help teach certain concepts. Of course, you do not have to keep all of these items on hand. These suggestions, however, should help you accumulate an interesting and varied collection of your own.

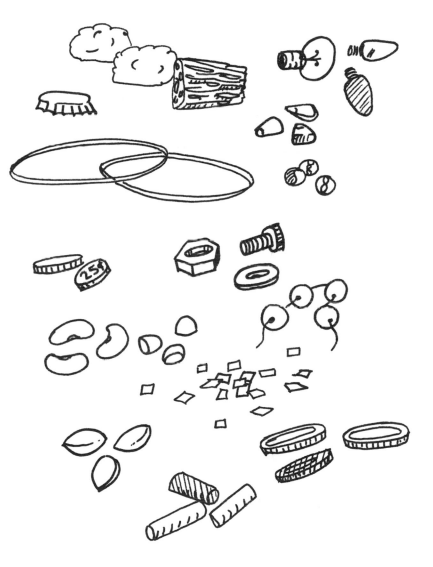

Acetate, colored	Bottle caps	Cigar bands
Acorns	Bottles	Cigarette wrappers
Acorn tops	Boxes	Clock parts
Allspice	Brads	Clothespins
Almonds	Braiding	Cloth scraps
Aluminum foil	Broken parts	Cloves
Apple seeds	Broken toys	Coffee filters
Apricot seeds	Buckles	Coffee grounds
	Buckram	Coins
Ball bearings	Burlap scraps	Combs, broken
Balsa wood		Confetti
Bamboo	Cancelled stamps	Construction paper
Bark	Candles	scraps
Basket reeds	Candy wrappers	Contact paper
Beads	Cardboard scraps	Cord
Beans	Carpet samples	Corks
Belts	Carpet warp	Corn husks
Bias tape	Cellophane scraps	Corn kernels
Blotter paper	Cellophane tape	Costume jewelry
Bobby pins	Chains	Cotton batting
Bolts and nuts	Chalk	Cotton puffs
Bones	Checkers	Crepe paper scraps

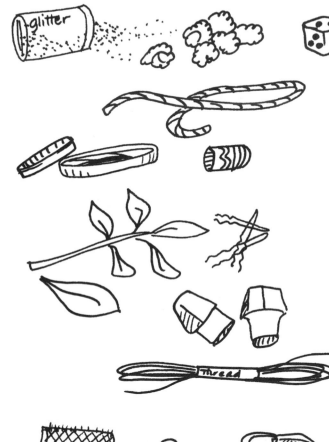

Crystals

Dice
Dominoes
Drapery samples
Dried beans and
   peas
Dried flowers and
   grasses
Dried seeds
Driftwood
Dry cereals

Easter grass
Egg cartons
Eggshells
Elastic
Emery boards
Embroidery thread
Erasers
Evergreens
Eyelets
Excelsior

Fabrics
Faucet washers
Feathers
Felt scraps
Film spools
Filters
Fish tank gravel
Fishing lures,
   hooks removed
Flashbulbs, used
Flint paper

Flocking
Florist's foil, foam,
   tape
Flowers, artificial
Flowers, dried
Foam packing of
   many shapes
Fur samples

Gauze
Gift wrap paper
Gimp nails
Glass beads
Glass mosaic rocks
   and pieces
Glitter
Gold thread
Gold jewelry parts
Grains
Gravel
Gummed labels
Gummed notebook
   paper reinforcers
Gummed paper

Hair netting
Hairpins
Hair rollers
Hardware scraps
Hat trimmings
Hooks

Ice cream sticks
Inner tube scraps

Jewelry pieces
Jewelry wire
Junk of all kinds
Jute

Key rings
Key tabs
Keys

Lace
Laminated items
Leather scraps
Leaves
Lentils
Lids
Linoleum scraps

Macaroni
Mailing tubes
Map pins
Marbles
Masonite
Meat trays, paper
Meat trays,
   Styrofoam
Meat trays, trans-
   parent plastic
Metal scraps
Metal shavings
Mirrors
Mosquito netting
Moss, dried

Nails
Newspapers

Noodles, dry
Noodles, wet
Nut cups
Nuts

Oilcloth scraps
Orange seeds
Orange sticks
Origami paper
Ornaments

Paint chips
Paper baking cups
Paper clips
Paper dots from
    computer paper
Paper fasteners
Paper products of
    all kinds
Paper tubes
Pebbles
Pill bottles
Pillboxes
Pinecones
Pine needles
Ping-Pong balls
Pins of all kinds
Pipe cleaners
Pits
Plastic bottles
Plastic foam
Plastic scraps
Popcorn
Potatoes
Pumpkin seeds

Q-tips
Quartz crystals
Quills

Raffia
Recording tape
Rhinestones
Ribbons
Rice
Rickrack
Rock salt
Rocks
Rope pieces
Rubber bands
Rubber tubing

Safety pins
Salt crystals
Sandpaper
Sawdust
Scouring pads
Screening,
    plastic or wire
Screws
Seals, gummed
Seam binding
Seashells
Seedpods
Seeds
Sequins
Sewing tape
Shoe laces
Shot
Silk scraps
Skewers, wooden

Soap
Soldering wire
Spaghetti
Sponges
Spools
Spray can lids
Stamps, savings
Stars, gummed
Steel wool
Sticks
Stones
Straws, broom
Straws, drinking
String
Styrofoam

Tape, cellophane
Tape, masking
Tape, mystic
Tape, plastic
Tape, Scotch
Tape, sewing
Telephone wire
Thistles
Threads
Tiles
Tinkertoy parts
Tissue paper
    scraps
Tongue depressors
Toothbrushes
Toothpicks
Torn paper scraps
Twigs
Twine

Typewriter ribbon
  spools

Velvet scraps
Velveteen
Vermiculite

Wallpaper

Warp
Washers
Wax candles
Weeds
Wood scraps
Wood shavings
Wooden beads
Wooden dowels

Wooden wheels
Wool
Wrapping papers

X-ray plates

Yarns
Zippers

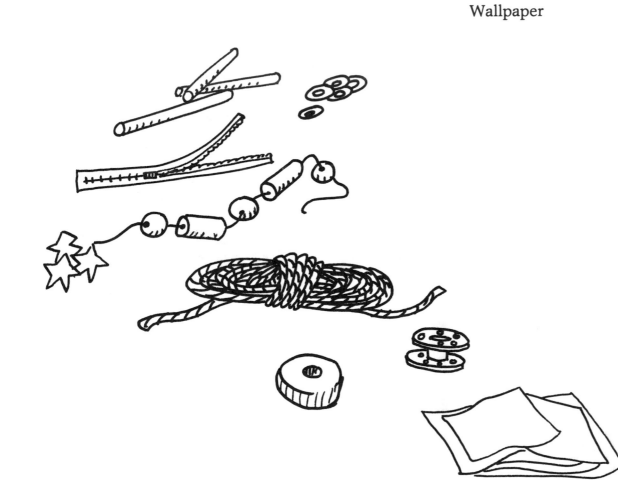

PRESSED NATURE

MATERIALS:
1. dried, pressed grasses, ferns, flowers, weeds
2. newspaper
3. books or weights
4. glue
5. paper

PROCESS:
1. press grasses, ferns, etc., between newspaper weighted with books for one week
2. glue these dried pieces on your choice of paper

VARIATIONS:
glue on:

fabric	note cards
styrofoam grocery tray	laminate between wax
block of wood	paper
driftwood	press between clear
rock	contact paper
wax paper	under glass in a frame

TISSUE PAPER ON WOOD OR GLASS

MATERIALS:
1. liquid starch or a glue/water mixture
2. art tissue scraps and squares
3. pieces of wood, jars, bottles, rocks, etc.
4. paint brush
5. newspaper

PROCESS:
1. using liquid starch or a mixture of glue and water, brush tissue pieces onto wood, glass, rocks, or bottles
2. be sure to stick down all edges
3. overlap edges
4. dry
5. spray with clear enamel if you like

VARIATIONS:
1. a design can be made, an actual scene, or small squares
2. torn edges are effective
3. nice for stained glass hangings in windows on wax paper
4. incorporate magazine letters
5. try on a framed piece of glass to hang in a window

ART TISSUE AND CLEAR CONTACT PAPER

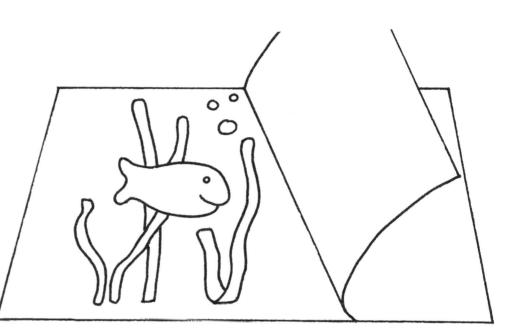

MATERIALS:

1. clear contact paper cut in workable size, such as 8x10
2. art tissue squares and scraps

PROCESS:

1. pull back *half* of protective backing on contact paper
2. press or fold it down
3. place pieces of art tissue on the sticky uncovered side of the contact paper
4. tissue may be torn or cut
5. work for scenes, designs, or patterns
6. pull remaining protective backing off
7. fold this half over the design and press with hands
8. trim edges, round corners

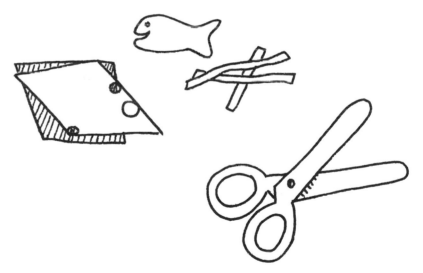

VARIATIONS:

1. punch with paper punch and tie string for hanging
2. use in windows, use in mobiles
3. press other items into the design such as dry weeds, flowers, doilies, lace, crayon shavings, glitter, feathers, and other ideas from your imagination

TISSUE DYE

MATERIALS:
1. water, small cups
2. food coloring or powdered fabric dye
3. white wrapping tissue
4. newspaper or drying rack

PROCESS:
1. mix small cups of water with several drops of food coloring (powdered fabric dye from art stores is very bright and has many choices of color)
2. fold white wrapping tissue in any shape
3. dip edges or points into color (dipping more than one color creates lovely effects)
4. allow to dry before unfolding, on newspaper, or a wooden drying rack (drying time can be shortened by placing tissue in a warm oven or in a microwave)
5. unfold
6. press with iron if desired

VARIATIONS:
1. these papers make a nice gift when folded and tied with a ribbon
2. use for wrapping paper
3. tape in a sunny window
4. drymount to posterboard and display as a poster or picture
5. dip napkins, paper towels, coffee filters

STYROFOAM TRAY WEAVING

MATERIALS:
1. clean, styrofoam grocery tray
2. scissors
3. yarns, fabrics, feathers, straw, etc.
4. tape

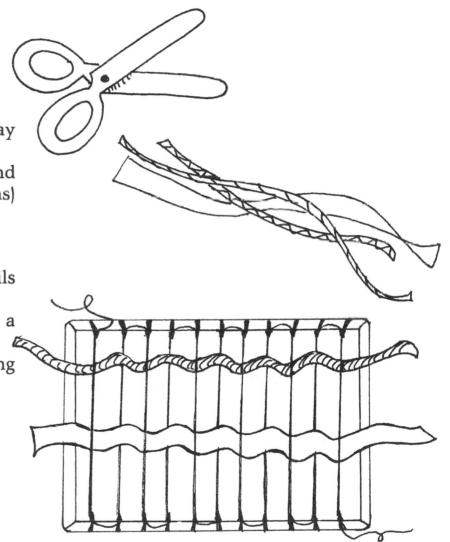

PROCESS:
1. string yarn back and forth through cuts on foam tray (cuts are made at top edge and bottom edge)
2. weave yarns, fabrics, feathers, or any items on hand through the strings (experiment with weaving patterns)
3. tape end of yarn to back of tray, or tie in a knot

VARIATIONS:
1. try this same technique on a block of wood with nails to string yarn back and forth; then weave
2. use a variety of sizes of trays or wood to achieve a variety of weavings
3. try sewing many weavings together for a large hanging

STYROFOAM TRAY STITCHERY

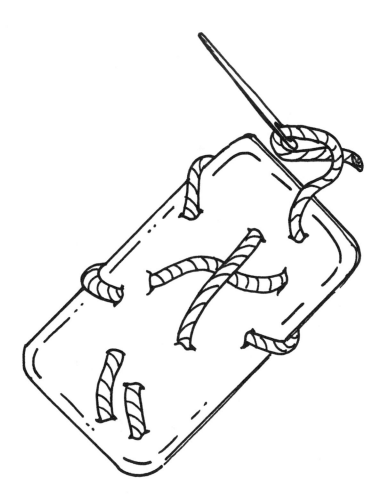

MATERIALS:
1. clean, styrofoam grocery tray
2. pencil, scissors, or hole punch
3. large plastic darning needle or tape
4. yarn

PROCESS:
1. punch holes in tray with scissors, pencil, or hole punch
2. push yarn through holes, knotting or taping end to make a "needle" (a plastic darning needle also works)
3. tape or tie end of yarn on back to finish

HINT:
1. for young children, use many short pieces of yarn instead of one long one to prevent tangling

VARIATIONS:
1. using a large plastic needle, "sew" on tray with yarn without pre-punching holes
2. try this technique on burlap, fabric, paper, cardboard
3. change colors, threads, sewing trims, fibers, etc.
4. stick in feathers, wools, cotton balls, etc.
5. cut slits in sides of trays and "wrap" yarn instead of sewing
6. cut slits in sides of cardboard and "wrap yarn"

recipes and formulas

RECIPES AND FORMULAS

BUBBLE PRINT
A solution of equal parts water and dish detergent.

CORNSTARCH AND BAKING SODA
Combine: 1 C. cornstarch, 2 cups baking soda, 1¼ C. water in a pan over medium heat, stirring constantly until thick like dough.
Food coloring may be worked in when cooled slightly, on a breadboard or on a piece of foil.
Keep covered.
Roll, cut, model in small shapes.

CORNSTARCH AND SALT DOUGH
Mixture: 1 C. salt, 1 C. cornstarch, ½ C. boiling water, and food coloring or tempera.
Mix over low heat, stirring until mixture is too stiff to stir.
When cool, knead until smooth. Model. Dry. Paint.

EASEL PAINT THAT LASTS

Add: Bentonite Extender to powdered tempera paint for an excellent easel paint.

To make:

1 cup Bentonite (available in powder form at most art stores)

½ C. soap powder

2 quarts water

Mix well with an eggbeater, food processor, blender.

Let stand in a plastic or ceramic container for 2-3 days, stirring once each day.

For the paint:

Mix 6-8 T. extender with a 1 lb. container of powdered tempera, 3 C. liquid starch, 2 T. soap flakes and a little water.

Store in a tightly covered container, pouring out what you need for each paint session.

ALSO: MORE IDEAS! Mix powdered tempera paint with:

1. water and soap to make it more washable
2. detergent to prevent cracking
3. liquid starch to make it thicker
4. sawdust, eggshells, coffee grounds, etc., to give texture

FINGERPAINTS: 2 recipes

1. mix liquid starch and powdered tempera paint on the paper as you paint
2. mix paste or liquid starch, 1 or 2 T. soap flakes, and food coloring or powdered tempera paint together in a bowl. Then whip with a beater. Fill small containers with paste or starch mixture, adding more food coloring or powdered paint for bright color.

GLUE, THINNED

Squeeze some white glue into a jar or dish and mix in water with a paint brush until it is thin and "paints" easily.

PLAY DOUGH

(There are many recipes, but this one has been fool proof for me for many years.)

Mix and cook on LOW in pan until ball forms. Then knead.

1 cup flour	1 T. cream of tartar
1 cup water	leave natural or color with:
1 cup salt	food coloring, tempera, kool-aid, jello

SAWDUST MODELING

Mix: 4 C. sawdust, 1 C. wheat paste, 2½ C. water
    color optional

SALT AND FLOUR BEADS
Mix: 1 C. salt, 1 C. flour, 1 T. alum
       mix to consistency of putty with water (add tempera
       or food coloring for color)
       pinch off and shape

SCRIBBLE COOKIES
1. save stub ends of old crayons and break in pieces
2. sort in muffin tins
3. placc in warm oven which has been turned off
4. let melt, and then cool
5. pop out

SUGAR WATER FOR BRIGHTER CHALK
Mix: ½ C. water, 2 T. sugar
       Stir until dissolved.
       Dip chalk into sugar water and color. Bright. Less
       smudgy.

TURPENTINES
1. pour water into a shallow tray
2. in separate cups, mix turpentine with powdered
   tempera (mix to a bright, thin consistency)
3. dribble paint mixture onto surface of water, swirling
   and mixing patterns with a stick or spoon

notes

BIBLIOGRAPHY

Barrata-Lorton, Mary. WORKJOBS FOR PARENTS. Menlo Park, CA: Addison-Wesley, 1975.

Bos, Bev. BEFORE THE BASICS. Roseville, CA: Turn the Page Press, 1983.

Brashears, Deya. ART EXPERIENCES FOR YOUNG CHILDREN. Walnut Creek, CA: Starlite Printing, 1984.

Cherry, Clare. CREATIVE ART FOR THE DEVELOPING CHILD. Belmont, CA: Fearon-Pitman, 1972.

Haas, Carolyn Buhai. THE BIG BOOK OF RECIPES FOR FUN. Northfield, IS: cgh publishing inc., 1980.

PAPER ART. Racine, WI: Whitman Publishing Company, 1966.

PRINT ART. Racine, WI: Whitman Publishing Company, 1966.

Wankelman, Willard F., Wigg, Philip, and Wigg, Marietta. A HANDBOOK OF ARTS AND CRAFTS. Dubuque, IA: Wm. C. Brown Company Publishers, 1968.

ABOUT THE AUTHOR

MaryAnn has an extensive background in teaching young children from pre-school through grade 3 with an individualized learning center approach based on language experience. She offers workshops and seminars on teaching effectively and enjoyably with a child-centered curriculum. She has a B.S. in Elementary Education from Old Dominion University, Virginia, and graduate studies at Western Washington University in speech, drama and teaching the creative arts.

Presently MaryAnn is consulting in the schools on creative art, illustrating, dramatics, and helping young authors with their projects. She is a frequent guest speaker at educational conferences and workshops, working with teachers and parents of all aged children on how to allow children their creativity.

Another book by the author is *MUDWORKS: Creative Clay, Dough, and Modeling Experiences*, 1989.

Watch for more BRIGHT IDEAS FOR LEARNING CENTERS by MaryAnn in the future.